GOURMET LONDON

Written by
William Skidelsky

Illustrated by
Alain Bouldouyre

AUTHENTIK BOOKS
Les Editions du Mont-Tonnerre
4 bis Villa du Mont-Tonnerre
Paris XVe arrondissement

Published by The Globe Pequot Press
246 Goose Lane, P.O. Box 480
Guilford, Connecticut 06437
www.globepequot.com

© 2007 Authentik Books
www.authentikbooks.com

Produced in France by Les Editions du Mont-Tonnerre
Text and illustrations copyright © Wilfried LeCarpentier

Authentik® Trademark, Wilfried LeCarpentier
4 bis Villa du Mont-Tonnerre, Paris XVe arrondissement
www.monttonnerre.com

ISBN 978-0-7627-4635-4
First Edition

Printed and bound in China

LES EDITIONS DU MONT-TONNERRE
Founder and Publisher: Wilfried LeCarpentier
Editor at Large: William Landmark
Managing Editor: Caroline Favreau

AUTHENTIK GOURMET LONDON
Restaurants, Wine and Food Consultant: Gérard Poirot
Project Editor: Nicola Mitchell
Project Editor: Jessica Fortescue
Copy Editors: Helen Stuart and Natasha Edwards
Proofreaders: Alison Culliford, Carly Jane Lock and Sandra Iskander
Researcher: Jessica Phelan
Editorial Assistant: Jennifer Parker

Creative Director: Lorenzo Locarno
Artistic Director: Nicolas Mamet
Graphic Designer: Amélie Dommange
Layout Artist: Marie-Thérèse Gomez
Cover Design and Packaging: Nicolas Mamet
Cartographer: Map Resources
Map Illustrator: Kouakou
Pre-Press and Production: Studio Graph'M, Paris

GLOBE PEQUOT PRESS
President and Publisher: Scott Watrous
Editorial Director: Karen Cure

ACKNOWLEDGEMENTS

Special thanks to Marie-Christine Levet, Scott Watrous, Karen Cure, Gunnar Stenmar, Gérard Paulin, Pierre Jovanovic, Jacques Derey, Bruno de sa Moreira, Ian Irvine, Laura Tennant, Francesco Betti and Charles Walker

Uncover the Exceptional

The Authentik book collection was born out of a desire to explore beauty and craftsmanship in every domain and in whatever price bracket. The books describe the aesthetic essence of a city, homing in on modern-day artisans who strive for perfection and whose approach to their work is as much spiritual as commercial. Written by specialist authors, the guides delve deep into the heart of a capital and, as a result, are excellent companions for both locals and nomadic lovers of fine living. Their neat size, made to fit into a suit or back pocket, make them easy and discreet to consult, and their elegant design and insider selection of addresses will ensure that you get to the heart of the local scene and blend in perfectly with it. There is even a notebook at the back for some cerebral scribbling of your own. In all, Authentik Books are the perfect accessory for uncovering the exceptional, whether in the arts, fashion, design or gastronomy.

Wilfried LeCarpentier
Founder and Publisher

Contents

How to Use This Guide

Ever felt like jumping in a black cab at Heathrow and saying, "Take me to the centre of things!?" Well, this book does the work of a very knowledgeable cab driver.

Gourmet London consists of ten chapters of insider information on the city's culinary scene. It steers you to the finest restaurants and gourmet neighbourhoods; quotes celebrity chefs on their favourite food and wine shops; gives advice on the best cookery schools such as Le Cordon Bleu and Leiths for honing your own repertoire of recipes; and recommends the best kitchen and tableware stores.

The directory at the end of each chapter gives the addresses of the places mentioned as well as other essential stops too numerous to mention in the chapter. The maps at the back of the guide cover the principal streets of central London. Use the map references following the addresses to find the general location of our listings.

Using the **2D BAR CODE** below you can load all the addresses onto a mobile phone with Internet access. This unique aspect of the book enables you to travel extra light.

scan here

How to access content on your mobile phone

If your mobile phone has Internet access and a built-in camera go to

www.scanlife.com

Download the free software that allows your mobile phone to identify the bar code. Downloading takes less than one minute. Then go to your personal file icon which will appear on your phone's menu screen, and select the icon **Scanlife**. Next, point your camera at the 2D bar code. A sound confirms that the bar code has been recognized. You can then access the directories on your phone.

A CULINARY WORLD
IN ONE CITY

The Wolseley
160 Piccadilly, W1

Previous page: Borough Market
8 Southwark St, SE1

I f you're sophisticated, solvent and a lover of fine food in all its variety, then there are few better places to live, or visit, than London. These days, Britain's capital offers numerous temptations to gourmets, from innovative restaurants and food shops to vibrant cafés and bustling street markets. This hasn't always been the case. Until fairly recently, London (and indeed Britain as a whole) was considered a gastronomic backwater, especially when compared to other European countries such as France and Italy. But today many would agree with *Gourmet* magazine's verdict that London is the "gourmet capital of the world."

Strength in diversity

When people are asked to sum up London's gastronomic appeal, the word they invariably use is "variety" and this is indeed the key to the city's success: London's food scene is extraordinarily diverse. Barcelona may have better tapas bars, Paris may have better patisseries, New York may have better steakhouses, but what makes London special is that it has great tapas bars, patisseries *and* steakhouses, and lots more besides. There are first-rate French, Italian and Spanish restaurants nestled side by side with superb sushi bars and dim sum parlours.

Breakfasting in the capital

Somerset Maugham once said, "If you want to eat well in England, you have to eat breakfast three times a day." While that is definitely no longer true, English breakfasts can be a real delight. Always go for British bacon – **Duchy Originals** *(see page 82)* is a good bet, while **The Ginger Pig** *(see page 127)* is a must for pork sausages. Finding a good quality breakfast out and about is easier in London than anywhere else in the world. Try Oliver Peyton's **Inn the Park** *(see page 131)*, where the 'freestyle' breakfast menu allows you to choose from five types of bacon, five types of sausage, three types of black pudding, and so on. The Wolseley *(see page 43)* is a haven for breakfast, whether in true British, French or American style, as is **Claridge's** *(see page 61)*. For breakfast that's less of an investment try **Raoul's** at 13 Clifton Road, W9, or 105 Talbot Road, W11, where health-reviving smoothies come hand-in-hand with a full gamut of breakfasting possibilities. There is also the excellent **Butcher & Grill** *(see page 41)* in Clapham. For an East London morning feast, try **Smiths of Smithfield** or **The Hope** *(see page 41)*; you won't need lunch.

Far-flung glamour

In London you can experience the kind of luxurious gastronomic cuisine more usually associated with Paris at **Le Gavroche**, **Gordon Ramsay** and **L'Atelier de Joël Robuchon** or the glitz and glamour normally linked with New York at **Nobu** and **The Ivy**. There is an impressive ethnic scene: some of the most glamorous restaurants in the capital these days are Indian, Chinese and Japanese, such as **Benares**, **China Tang** and **Umu**. Mexican, Korean, even Afghan, food has been getting in on the act. And let's not forget that British cooking is making a comeback, led by the trailblazing **St John**. No other city in the world can boast such diversity.

Home cooking

Restaurants, however, are only part of the story. The ingredients on offer in London have seen improvements across the board, too. Gone are the days when you'd struggle to find a decent cup of coffee or sandwich: smart new delis and cafés have been springing up all over town. Londoners increasingly love to cook at home and, as a result, even a modest corner shop will often sell fresh basil, sticks of lemongrass or vanilla pods alongside the sliced white bread.

L'Atelier de Joël Robuchon
3-15 West St, WC2

Artisan revival

Supermarkets are better than they once were, but Londoners are increasingly obtaining their food from other sources. There is a thriving farmers market scene and high-end shopping destinations such as **Borough Market** are immensely popular. Artisan traditions are being rediscovered: London nowadays is home to almost as many bakers, cake-makers, and chocolatiers as Paris. Perhaps there aren't as many butchers and fishmongers as there could be – but excellent ones can be found.

Cookery classes and wine courses are Londoners' latest obsession, and demand is surging for quality cooking equipment and creative tableware. In just about every area you can imagine, London's culinary scene has burst into life.

Culinary cognoscenti

With this new interest in food and eating has come a transformation in the status of chefs. While cooking was once seen as a lowly trade, today's most successful chefs are household names. Figures such as Gordon Ramsay, Jamie Oliver and Marco Pierre White are just as likely to make the headlines as athletes and film stars. The food scene in London, in fact, can sometimes seem as if it is about more than just food: it has

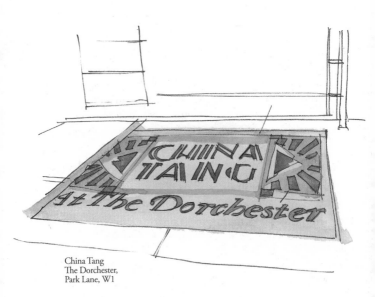

China Tang
The Dorchester,
Park Lane, W1

become bound up with lifestyle and aspiration, with celebrity and wealth. One effect of this has been to make those who comment on it almost as important as the protagonists themselves. Leading restaurant critics such as A. A. Gill (*The Sunday Times*) and Fay Maschler (*The Evening Standard*) are read avidly, and a single review can help determine whether a restaurant succeeds.

London's culinary renaissance has naturally been the work of many: restaurant owners, shopkeepers, producers and consumers. But at its centre is a small group of pioneering individuals – both British and nonnative – who have led the way in transforming the capital's culinary life. Gordon Ramsay, inevitably, heads the list. Foul-mouthed and precociously talented (and already tagged by the food guides before he was 30), Ramsay now presides over a global haute cuisine empire that includes many of London's finest restaurants.

Less familiar, but in her way no less important, is Henrietta Green, who has been the driving force behind the farmers market movement. Largely thanks to her, most areas of town have weekly markets at which shoppers can buy directly from producers. The Chinese entrepreneur Alan Yau has popularized Japanese and Thai cuisine in the last decade with his hugely successful **Wagamama** and **Busaba Eathai** chains; he is

Yauatcha
15 Broadwick St, W1

now doing the same for high-end Chinese dining with **Hakkasan** and **Yauatcha**. And it is impossible to ignore Jamie Oliver, the *Naked Chef* of his own TV series, who runs an apprentice scheme for deprived teenagers at his restaurant **Fifteen**, and who has led a campaign to improve the diets of British children.

Books for cooks

Perhaps the single most influential restaurant in the capital has been the **River Café**. When Rose Gray and Ruth Rogers opened it in 1987, they introduced Londoners to a new kind of eating: simple food based on superb ingredients served in a relaxed, open-plan setting. This approach has inspired countless other restaurants, and has hugely influenced the way British people cook at home.

In the 1990s, Gray and Rogers' series of River Café cookbooks became gastronomic bibles for scores of affluent Londoners, who embraced with relief the novel idea that cooking well needn't involve expert technical knowledge and hours of preparation. More recently, **Moro**'s two cookbooks have replaced the River Café books as the standard textbooks for London entertaining – but, seeing as its authors, husband and wife team Sam and Sam Clarke, started out at the River Café, the influence of Gray and Rogers lives on.

The Ivy
1-5 West Street, WC2

Back to British roots

The food scene that has emerged in London over the past decade is a unique combination of styles and influences, a mix of the homegrown and the exotic, the traditional and the radical. London's poor culinary record has, strangely, been an advantage of sorts. Lacking a strong native food culture to draw on, British chefs have looked abroad for inspiration. But their success in doing so has, paradoxically, given them the confidence to start reinvestigating their own country's traditions. Perhaps the biggest benefit of London's emergence as a major food city will be Britain's rediscovery of its own culinary roots.

01

St John
26 St John St, EC1

RESTAURANTS,
CAFES AND BARS

The Providores
109 Marylebone High St, W1

Previous page: Maison Bertaux
28 Greek St, W1

L ondon has a huge, some would even say bewildering, number of great restaurants. The good news is that finding most of them isn't too challenging. The best ones tend to be in, or near, the centre. Recently, good places have started opening up in such far-flung destinations as south London (previously a virtually gourmet-free zone). However, you can stay within a relatively small area and not deprive yourself unduly.

Back to basics

Restaurant cooking in London these days tends to be up-to-the-minute without being overly experimental. You won't find too many examples of molecular gastronomy, although this can be sampled at the **Fat Duck** in Bray near Windsor; nor will you find much fusion cooking, save the rare exception of the excellent **The Providores** in Marylebone. The trend has been towards a plainer, more authentic style: these days it is enough for chefs to produce successful versions of individual countries' cuisines to draw in the crowds.

Bibendum
Michelin House
81 Fulham Rd, SW3

Haute cuisine and French finesse

The lion's share of the city's luxurious restaurants are, not surprisingly, in the affluent west London boroughs of Mayfair, Knightsbridge, Kensington and Chelsea. Most of these gastronomically acclaimed places serve classical French haute cuisine. Leading the field is **Gordon Ramsay** – the artistic foodie's favourite and a gastronomic shrine to rival any in the world. Be prepared to wait weeks, even months, for a table. If you can't get one, consider the other London restaurants in Ramsay's ever-expanding empire: **Gordon Ramsay at Claridge's**, **Petrus**, **La Noisette**, **Angela Hartnett at the Connaught**, **Maze**, the (British) **Savoy Grill** and **The Narrow**.

Although each has a different head chef, all are consistent with the Ramsay ethos: classic, pure flavours, lightness of touch, and attention to detail. Many offer the chance to dine at a special chef's table in the kitchen, a great way to pick up some secret cooking tips *(see Chapter Seven)*.

02

Eccentric settings

Sarastro
126 Drury Lane, WC2

Some restaurants are not so much about food as concept. London has various options for diners who crave novelty and eccentricity.

At **Dans Le Noir**, in Clerkenwell, you eat your meal entirely in the dark – an experience that sounds scary but is surprisingly fun.

Les Trois Garçons serves excellent French food, but its real attraction is its wonderful theatrical decor – vintage handbags dangle from the ceiling and exotic stuffed animals line the walls.

At **Sarastro**, in Covent Garden, diners eat in individually styled boxes while being serenaded by singers from the nearby Royal Opera House.

Other classical French highlights include **Le Gavroche** (run by the Roux family for four decades, and still as superb as ever), **The Capital** (where Eric Chavot presides) and Philip Howard's faultless **The Square**. For more cutting-edge food – though still obviously French both **Pied à Terre** in Fitzrovia and **Tom Aikens** in Chelsea are excellent, as is **Sketch**, the adventurous outlet of Paris chef Pierre Gagnaire; try, too, **Chez Bruce** in Wandsworth. **Galvin at Windows** is a pleasure both for its sumptuous modern French cuisine and its 28th-floor view over Hyde Park. The Galvin bistro also has an address in Marylebone. Staying within the haute cuisine category, but moving away from France, **The Greenhouse** in Mayfair offers some of the most exciting modern European cooking in the capital.

02

Italian gourmet

There is no shortage of first-rate Italian restaurants. **Locanda Locatelli** not only serves great food but is one of London's most popular celebrity venues. The path-forging **River Café**, opened in 1987, has never deviated from its winning formula of exquisite ingredients, simply prepared. **Alloro** in Mayfair is great for modern Italian food; the more traditional **Zafferano** in Knightsbridge is also a must. If you're in the West End, a good choice is the popular **Orso**, which offers inventive, aromatic Italian dishes.

Moro
34-36 Exmouth Market, EC1

Hispanic flair

Spanish food, for a long time poorly represented in London, finally seems to be breaking through. **Moro** (which, strictly speaking, is southern Spanish and North African) is a well-established favourite. There are also some excellent tapas bars, including **Tapas Brindisa**, **Fino**, **Salt Yard** and **Tendido Cero**. Try, too, **Cigala** in Bloomsbury. South American restaurants are the latest dining trend in the capital. For succulent Argentinian steak, go to **Gaucho Grill** (there are seven branches).

02

Asian and Indian aromas

One of the most significant culinary developments since 2000 has been the emergence of high-end Asian cooking capable of rivalling, and in many cases surpassing, the European food on offer. Some of the best Japanese cooking (along with serious glitz) is to be found at **Nobu**; **Zuma**, **Umu** and **Roka** are also first rate. Refined Indian cooking has come on apace in the past decade: good examples are **Benares**, **Rasoi Vineet Bhatia** and **Tamarind**.

For sophisticated Chinese cooking in a spectacular setting, **Hakkasan** is hard to beat; for dim sum try **Yauatcha** or **Royal China**. **Bar Shu** in Soho focuses on Sichuan cuisine and is well worth a visit – although be careful, as the dishes can be mouth-numbingly hot.

Modern British

British food is strongly represented these days. Fergus Henderson, chef at **St John**, has rightly been acclaimed for his gutsy, adventurous style: no one in the world can have done more to raise the profile of offal. A more rarefied take on the nation's culinary traditions can be found at Richard Corrigan's **Lindsay House**; and **Roast** in Borough Market does great modern British cooking – it also serves an excellent breakfast *(see also page 14)*. For real pomp and ceremony, try the **Goring Hotel** in Victoria.

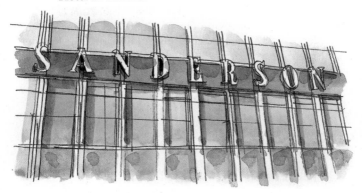

Long Bar at Sanderson
50 Berners St, W1

Cafés and tea rooms

Cafés in London are getting better all the time. The quirkily charming Soho fixture, **Maison Bertaux**, serves good traditional patisserie. **Ladurée** in Harrods is as elegant as its Parisian counterpart and **La Fromagerie** in Marylebone offers an excellent range of British snacks. **The Wolseley** on Piccadilly presents an enticing mix of British cakes and French patisserie. For something really out of the ordinary, try the tea room at dim sum specialist **Yauatcha**: the strange-looking cakes are amazing, and there are around 150 varieties of tea.

02

Bar culture

London's bar scene, although still not quite a match for New York's, shouldn't be overlooked. **Hakkasan** does delicious Oriental-inspired cocktails in a spectacular setting. **Hawksmoor**, in east London, mixes great classic cocktails. It is also doubles up as an excellent steak restaurant). The **Long Bar** at the Philippe Starck-designed Sanderson hotel is aggressively stylish. **Salt Whisky Bar** near Marble Arch is, as its name suggests, the place for whisky with over 200 tipples to sample. The bar at **China Tang**, in The Dorchester hotel, is a favourite hangout of the rich and famous. For really over-the-top decor and a decadent setting, head for **Annex 3** near Oxford Circus.

Good value gastro

London's restaurants are undoubtedly expensive: in most cases, if you want really good food, you have to pay dearly for it. Nonetheless, fine dining and just a medium-sized dent in one's wallet are not incompatible – although in some cases it requires travelling from the centre. More modestly priced gastronomic fare can be sampled at **Arbutus** in Soho, while **Canteen** in Spitalfields serves a very good classic British menu at very reasonable prices with main courses under £10.

Gastro pubs are another good way of sampling modern British food fairly cheaply, and the **Anchor & Hope** in Waterloois notable. While tables are a bit of a lottery, as you can't book, the **Marquess Tavern** in Islington and the **Pig's Ear** in Chelsea, are both worth a visit. Gordon Ramsay, not a man usually associated with budget dining, has also ventured into the gastro pub field with **The Narrow** in east London.

Reliably good and moderately priced Thai and Japanese food is available at Alan Yau's two flagship chains, **Busaba Eathai** and **Wagamama**, while if you want sushi on a budget, your best bet is **Sushi-Hiro** in Ealing. **Bi-Won**, in Bloomsbury, is one of the best of the capital's Korean cafés. The best budget option for lovers of Indian food is **Masala Zone**. Soho and Covent Garden are both full of perfectly good Italian trattorias, although for delicious, simple reasonably-priced Italian food, **Carluccio's** cafés *(see Chapter Three)* are hard to beat.

Fast but flavourful

02

Good-quality fast food is becoming more widely available in London. The trailblazer here is the restaurant and café chain **Leon**, whose four branches serve interesting dishes with an eastern Mediterranean slant, at a fraction of what you would pay in a smarter restaurant. Similar in concept is the outstanding **Hummus Bros**, which has created a surprising variety of dishes costing no more than £5 out of their Middle Eastern staple cuisine. London's thriving gourmet burger bar scene is also a boon to the budget conscious: of the many chains, **Gourmet Burger Kitchen** stands out.

Marquess Tavern
32 Canonbury St, N1

Haute cuisine and French finesse

Aubergine
11 Park Walk, SW10
⊖ South Kensington
ⓒ 020 7352 3449
auberginerestaurant.co.uk
⊕ 13/F17

**L'Atelier de Joël
Robuchon**
13-15 West St, WC2
⊖ Tottenham Ct Rd
ⓒ 020 7010 8600
⊕ 7/PG

Bibendum
81 Fulham Rd, SW3
⊖ South Kensington
ⓒ 020 781 5817
bibendum.co.uk
⊕ 13/F17

The Capital
22 Basil St, SW3
⊖ Knightsbridge
ⓒ 020 7589 5171
capital-london.net
⊕ 10/J13

Chez Bruce
2 Bellevue Rd, SW17
⊜ Wandsworth Common
ⓒ 020 8672 0114
chezbruce.co.uk
⊕ Off map

Club Gascon
57 West Smithfield, EC1
⊖ Barbican
ⓒ 020 7796 0600
clubgascon.com
⊕ 8/U7

Galvin at Windows
London Hilton,
22 Park Lane, W1
⊖ Hyde Park Corner
ⓒ 020 7208 4021
hilton.co.uk/londonparklane
⊕ 10/K10

Galvin Bistro de Luxe
66 Baker St, W1
⊖ Baker Street
ⓒ 020 7935 4007
galvinbistrodeluxe.co.uk
⊕ 6/K6

Gordon Ramsay
68 Royal Hospital Rd, SW3
⊖ Sloane Square
ⓒ 020 7352 4441
gordonramsay.com
⊕ 14/J16

The Greenhouse
27a Hay's Mews, W1
⊖ Green Park
ⓒ 020 7499 3331
greenhouserestaurant.co.uk
⊕ 11/M10

Le Gavroche
43 Upper Brook St, W1
⊖ Marble Arch
ⓒ 020 7408 0881
le-gavroche.co.uk
⊕ 6/K9

Pied à Terre
34 Charlotte St, W1
⊖ Goodge Street
ⓒ 020 7636 1178
pied-a-terre.co.uk
⊕ 7/N6

Sketch
9 Conduit St, W1
⊖Bond Street
ⓒ 0870 777 4488
sketch.uk.com
⊕ 6/M

The Square
6-10 Bruton St, W1
⊖ Green Park
ⓒ 020 7495 7100
squarerestaurant.com
⊕ 6/M9

Tom Aikens
43 Elystan St, SW3
⊖ South Kensington
ⓒ 020 7584 2003
tomaikens.co.uk
⊕ 14/I15

Italian gourmet

Alloro
19 Dover St, W1
Green Park
020 7495 4768
alloro-restaurant.co.uk
11/M10

Locanda Locatelli
8 Seymour St, W1
Marble Arch
020 7935 9088
locandalocatelli.com
6/J8

Orso
27 Wellington St, WC2
Covent Garden
020 7240 5269
orsorestaurant.com
7/Q9

River Café
Thames Wharf,
Rainville Rd, W6
Hammersmith
020 7386 4200
rivercafe.co.uk
Off map

St Alban
4-12 Lower Regent St, SW1
Piccadilly Circus
020 7499 8558
6-7/N9

Zafferano
15 Lowndes St, SW1
Knightsbridge
020 7235 5800
zafferanorestaurant.com
10/K13

02

Hispanic flair

Asia de Cuba
45 St Martin's Lane, WC2
Leicester Square
0871 2238011
asiadecuba-restaurant.com
7/P9

Cigala
54 Lamb's Conduit St,
WC1
Russell Square
020 7405 1717
cigala.co.uk
7/R6

Fino
33 Charlotte Street, W1
Goodge Street
020 7813 8010
finorestaurant.com
7/N6

Floridita
100 Wardour St, W1
Tottenham Court Rd
020 7314 4000
floriditalondon.com
7/O8

Gaucho Grill
25 Swallow St, W1
Piccadilly Circus
020 7734 4040
gaucho-grill.com
11/N10

Moro
34 Exmouth Market, EC1
Farringdon
020 7833 8336
moro.co.uk
4/T5

Salt Yard
54 Goodge St, W1
Goodge Street
020 7637 0657
saltyard.co.uk
7/O7

Tapas Brindisa
18-20 Southwark St, SE1
London Bridge
020 7357 8880
brindisa.com
12/V11

Tendido Cero
174 Old Brompton Rd, SW5
Gloucester Road
020 7370 3685
cambiodetercio.co.uk
13-14/G15

Asian and Indian aromas

Amaya
18 Motcomb St, SW1
⊖ Knightsbridge
© 0871 2238036
realindianfood.com
⊕ 10/K13

Bar Shu
28 Frith St, W1
⊖ Tottenham Court Rd
© 020 7287 8822
bar-shu.co.uk
⊕ 7/O8

Benares
12a Berkeley House,
Berkeley Square, W1
⊖ Green Park
© 020 7629 8886
benaresrestaurant.com
⊕ 11/M10

Chutney Mary
535 King's Rd, SW10
⊖ Sloane Square
© 020 7351 3113
realindianfood.com
⊕ 10/K14

Hakkasan
8 Hanway Place, W1
⊖ Tottenham Court Rd
© 020 7907 1888
⊕ 7/O7

Kai
65 South Audley St, W1
⊖ Bond Street
© 020 7493 8988
kaimayfair
⊕ 10/L10

Nobu
The Metropolitan,
19 Old Park Lane, W1
⊖ Hyde Park Corner
© 020 7447 4747
noburestaurants.com
⊕ 10/L11

Rasoi Vineet Bhatia
10 Lincoln St, SW3
⊖ Sloane Square
© 020 7225 1881
vineetbhatia.com
⊕ 14/J15

Roka
37 Charlotte St, W1
⊖ Goodge Street
© 020 7580 6464
rokarestaurant.com
⊕ 7/N6

Royal China
40 Baker St, W1
⊖ Baker Street
© 020 7487 4688
royalchinaclub.co.uk
⊕ 6/K6

Sushi-Hiro
1 Station Parade
Uxbridge Rd, W5
⊖ Ealing Common
© 020 8896 3175
⊕ Off map

Tamarind
20 Queen St, W1
⊖ Green Park
© 020 7629 3561
tamarindrestaurant.com
⊕ 10/L10

Umu
14 Bruton Place, W1
⊖ Bond Street
© 020 7499 8881
umurestaurant.com
⊕ 6/M9

Yauatcha
15 Broadwick St, W1
⊖ Oxford Circus
© 020 7494 8888
⊕ 7/O8

Zuma
5 Raphael St, SW7
⊖ Knightsbridge
© 020 7584 1010
zumarestaurant.com
⊕ 10/I12

Modern British

The Goring Hotel
Beeston Place
Grosvenor Gardens, SW1
⊖ Victoria
① 020 7396 9000
goringhotel.co.uk
⊕ 11/M13

Lindsay House
21 Romilly St, W1
⊖ Leicester Square
① 020 7439 0450
lindsayhouse.co.uk
⊕ 7/P9

Savoy Grill
The Savoy, Strand, WC2
⊖ Tottenham Court Rd
① 020 7592 1600
gordonramsay.com
⊕ 11/Q10

**Konstam at
the Prince Albert**
2 Acton St, WC1
⊖ Russell Square
① 020 7833 5040
konstam.co.uk
⊕ 3/R4

Roast
The Floral Hall,
Borough Market,
Stoney St, SE1
⊖ London Bridge
① 020 7940 1300
roast-restaurant.com
⊕ 12/W11

St John
26 St John St, EC1
⊖ Farringdon
① 020 7251 0848
stjohnrestaurant.co.uk
⊕ 4/T4

02

Traditional British

The Butcher & Grill
39-41 Parkgate Rd, SW11
BR Clapham Junction
① 020 7924 3999
thebutcherandgrill.com
⊕ Off map

The Hope
94 Cowcross St, EC1
⊖ Farringdon
① 020 7253 8525
⊕ 8/U6

Simpson's-in-the-Strand
100 Strand, WC2
⊖ Embankment
① 020 7836 9112
fairmont.com/svy/simpson
⊕ 11/Q10

Sweetings
39 Queen Victoria St, EC4
⊖ Mansion House
① 020 7248 3062
⊕ 8/V9

**The Quality
Chop House**
94 Farringdon Rd, EC1
⊖ Farringdon
① 020 7837 5093
qualitychophouse.co.uk
⊕ 8/T6

Smiths of Smithfield
67 Charterhouse St, EC1
⊖ Farringdon
① 020 7251 7950
smithsofsmithfield.co.uk
⊕ 8/T7

Good value gastro

Anchor & Hope
36 The Cut, SE1
⊖ Southwark
ⓒ 020 7928 9898
⊕ 12/T12

Arbutus
63-64 Frith St, W1
⊖ Tottenham Court Rd
ⓒ 020 7734 4545.
arbutusrestaurant.co.uk
⊕ 7/O8

Bi-Won
24 Coptic St, WC1
⊖ Holborn
ⓒ 020 7580 2660
⊕ 7/P7

Busaba Eathai
106-110 Wardour St, W1
⊖ Tottenham Court Rd
ⓒ 020 7225 8686
⊕ 7/O8

Canteen
2 Crispin Place, E1
⊖ Liverpool Street
ⓒ 0845 6861 122
canteen.co.uk
⊕ 8/Z7

Fish!
Cathedral St, SE1
⊖ London Bridge
ⓒ 020 7407 3803
⊕ 12/W11

Gourmet Burger Kitchen
44 Northcote Rd, SW11
⊖ Clapham South
ⓒ 020 7228 3309
gbkinfo.com
⊕ Off map

Hummus Bros
88 Wardour St, W1
⊖ Leicester Square
ⓒ 020 7734 1311
hbros.co.uk
⊕ 7/O8

Leon
35 Great Marlborough St, W1
⊖ Oxford Circus
ⓒ 020 7437 5280
leonrestaurants.co.uk
⊕ 7/N8

Marquess Tavern
32 Canonbury St, N1
⊖ Highbury & Islington
ⓒ 020 7354 2975
themarquesstavern.co.uk
⊕ Off map

Masala Zone
80 Upper St, N1
⊖ Angel
ⓒ 020 7359 3399
realindianfood.com
⊕ 4/T2

The Narrow
44 Narrow St, E14
⊖ Shadwell
gordonramsay.com
⊕ Off map

Pig's Ear
35 Old Church St, SW3
⊖ Sloane Square
ⓒ 020 7352 2908
⊕ 13-14/G16

Sushi-Hiro
1 Station Parade,
Uxbridge Rd, W5
⊖ Ealing Common
ⓒ 020 8896 3175
⊕ Off map

Wagamama
4a Streatham St, WC1
⊖ Tottenham Court Rd
ⓒ 020 7323 9223
wagamama.com
⊕ 7/P7

Cafés, tea rooms and bars

Annex 3
6 Little Portland St, W1
⊖ Oxford Circus
℃ 020 7631 0700
annex3.co.uk
⊕ 7/N7

China Tang
The Dorchester
Park Lane, W1
⊖ Tottenham Court Rd
℃ 020 7629 9988
thedorchester.com
⊕ 10/L10

Hawksmoor
157 Commercial St, E1
⊖ Shoreditch
℃ 020 7247 7392
⊕ 8/Z6

Ladurée
Harrods, SW1
⊖ Knightsbridge
℃ 020 7730 1234
laduree.fr
⊕ 10/I13

La Fromagerie
2-4 Moxon St, W1
⊖ Regent's Park
℃ 020 7935 0341
lafromagerie.co.uk
⊕ 6/K7

Long Bar
The Sanderson,
50 Berners St, W1
⊖ Covent Garden
℃ 020 7300 1400
sandersonlondon.com
⊕ 7/N7

Maison Bertaux
28 Greek St, W1
⊖ Leicester Square
℃ 020 7437 6007
⊕ 7/P8

Salt Whisky Bar
82 Seymour St, W2
⊖ Marble Arch
℃ 020 7402 1155
saltbar.com
⊕ 6/J8

The Wolseley
160 Piccadilly, W1
⊖ Green Park
℃ 020 7499 6996
thewolseley.com
⊕ 11/M11

02

Eccentric settings

Dans Le Noir
30 Clerkenwell Green,
EC1
⊖ Farringdon
℃ 020 7253 1100
danslenoir.com
⊕ 4/T5

Les Trois Garçons
1 Club Row, E1
⊖ Shoreditch
℃ 020 7613 1924
lestroisgarcons.com
⊕ 4/Z5

Sarastro
126 Drury Lane, WC2
⊖ Covent Garden
℃ 020 7836 0101
sarastro-restaurant.com
⊕ 7/Q8

See page 9
to scan the
directory

GOURMET
NEIGHBOURHOODS

Battersea
Northcote Road, SW11

Previous page: Marylebone
High Street, W1

During the 17th, 18th and 19th centuries, London grew rapidly beyond its traditional boundaries, which corresponded roughly to those of Zone 1 of today's Tube map to take in outlying areas like Highgate, Hampstead, Camberwell and Battersea. Before being swallowed up, these areas were often no more than villages, and to this day many retain a local character. London may be a global megalopolis with a large and bustling centre, but it is also a city of neighbourhoods. It is impossible to do justice to London's food scene without considering how these fit into the picture.

03

Marylebone

One of the most charming of London's villages is Marylebone, which became a popular place for the well-heeled in the 17th and 18th centuries. Marylebone today pulls off the feat of combining the sleepiness of a Cotswold village with imposing Victorian and Georgian architecture and a wealth of boutiques. It is also a magnet for food lovers. Practically everything one could wish for is packed into this small area: a good supermarket, Waitrose, as well as numerous restaurants and cafés, bakers, butchers and delicatessens,

Kensington Church Street, W8

superb cookware shops, a Sunday farmers market and several cookery schools. Many of Marylebone's gourmet treasures are covered in other sections of this book. Of those that aren't, look out for the Belgian bakery and café **Le Pain Quotidien**, which has delicious sourdough loaves, cakes and tarts; the sausage shop **Biggles**, recommended for its *boerewors*, South African spiced sausage; and **Orrery Epicerie**, which sells excellent ready-made dishes as well as artisanal cheeses, charcuterie and bread. **Caffé Caldesi**, attached to the cookery school La Cucina Caldesi, is a good place to stop for a light lunch, while the French patisserie chain **Paul** does delicious ready-made sandwiches. Nearby is St Christopher's Place, a pedestrian alley with some excellent boutiques and restaurants. Also in the vicinity is the Wallace Collection, a museum that houses not only a superb collection of art, sculpture and antique armour but also a smart all-day French brasserie.

Notting Hill

Moving west from Marylebone, the next major gourmet stop is oh-so-fashionable Notting Hill. Once a draw for London's well-heeled bohemians – who were attracted as much by its stucco-fronted terrace houses as by its vibrant multicultural scene – Notting Hill is entirely gentrified today, yet still feels laid back. Kensington Church Street, just south of Notting Hill

Gate tube station, is home to the popular **Kensington Place** brasserie and the award-winning **Clarke's**. Both have shops attached: at Kensington Place a fishmonger, at Clarke's a wonderful bread and cake shop selling produce ranging from hand-rolled chocolate truffles to homemade mayonnaise and crisp, honeyed granola.

North of Notting Hill Gate, two thirds of the way up Portobello Road, is one of London's most bountiful food enclaves. This part of Portobello Road houses the food section of the famous Saturday market, where you will find good fruit and vegetables as well as numerous snacks, but its real attraction is its plethora of cafés, delis and unusual food shops.

In **Mr Christian's** delicatessen, for example, the tables and shelves groan with olives, breads, homemade brownies and flapjacks, pasta sauces and unusual oils and vinegars. Just opposite, **The Grocer on Elgin** is justly renowned for its restaurant-quality take-home meals; typical dishes include duck leg confit and braised beef in red wine and thyme. Around the corner, yet another deli, **Felicitous**, offers superb breads, cheeses, cakes and freshly prepared dishes. One road to the north is **Books for Cooks**, which stocks the most comprehensive range of cookbooks in London (and has a good café). The excellent Italian restaurant

Assaggi is not far away on Chepstow Place. Near the northern end of Portobello Road is Golborne Road, with its excellent Moroccan and Portuguese cafés and delis. Try **Le Maroc** and **Lisboa Delicatessen** as well as **Golborne Fisheries** *(see page 94)*.

Battersea and Clapham

Although South London has rarely been feted for its gourmet attractions, it doesn't lag far behind the north these days. The excellent Borough Market has helped put London Bridge and Bermondsey on the map, and several other neighbourhoods are also establishing their foodie credentials.

Northcote Road, in Battersea, stands out for its superb food shops. There is **A. Dove & Son**, a very good butcher; an excellent cheese shop, **Hamish Johnson**, with evocatively named varieties such as St Rothodon's Blue and Lincolnshire Poacher; the first rate Italian deli **I Sapori di Stefano Cavallini** – look for the artisanal ice creams made by Alba Gold; and the bread-stacked **Lighthouse Bakery**. Nearby Clapham is another emergent food destination: the impressive **M. Moen & Son** manages to combine the functions of butcher, deli and greengrocer. **Tsunami** on Voltaire Road is a Japanese restaurant to challenge the best.

Ethnic enclaves

London's ethnic communities have settled in neighbourhoods all across town, creating many enclaves of gastronomy. Chinatown, in the centre, contains a huge number of restaurants, but they are generally mediocre; you are better off heading to Soho and going to **Bar Shu**, **Yauatcha** or **Hakkasan** (*see page 33*).

Brick Lane is famous for its Bangladeshi curry houses, but in reality most of the food is poor; much better Indian food can be found in Tooting in south London – try **Kastoori** and **Radha Krishna Bhavan**. London's Turkish communities are concentrated around east London, and Dalston in particular has some first-rate *mangal* restaurants, focusing on grilled meat. Two standouts are **Mangal Ocakbasi** and **19 Numara Bos Cirrik**.

Just south of Dalston, on Kingsland High Street, is a strip of Vietnamese restaurants – **Sông Quê** and **Au Lac** are among the best. Some of the most delicious Middle Eastern food in London can be found around the Edgware Road; the excellent **Patogh**, for example, is a small Persian place that serves grilled meats with enormous discs of flatbread.

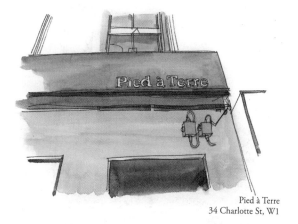

Pied à Terre
34 Charlotte St, W1

Fitzrovia

A few individual streets nearer the centre are notable for having a plethora of good restaurants. Charlotte Street in Fitzrovia, the heart of London's media land, has long been known as a restaurant destination. It even appears in Evelyn Waugh's novels as such, and Saul Bellow once wrote, "A man can be happy living on Charlotte Street." Today it has two really top notch places, **Pied à Terre** and **Roka**, alongside leading Hispanic restaurant **Fino** *(see Chapter Two)*. Others that are really very good are **Rasa Samudra** (southern Indian fish cookery), **Passione** (Italian), and the dependable steakhouse **Chez Gérard**.

Exmouth Market, EC1

Exmouth market

A new rival to Charlotte Street as London's top restaurant street is **Exmouth Market** in Farringdon, which not only has the famous **Moro** *(see page 33)*, and Spanish food shop **Brindisa**, but also **Medcalf** (gutsy British food), **Santore** (decent Italian) and the **Ambassador Café** (innovative modern European). It doesn't end there: around the corner, on Farringdon Street, is the **Quality Chop House** with funky, casual homely British classics such as shepherd's pie and one of London's landmark gastro pubs, the **Eagle**.

03

On the same stretch is the excellent budget restaurant **Little Bay**, which serves simple food at prices that, for London, seem impossibly reasonable. Exmouth Market also holds a small but top-notch farmers-style market on Friday and Saturday lunchtime – providing yet another incentive for a visit.

Claridge's
Brook Street, W1

Where to stay

London's gourmet neighbourhoods can also be interesting places to stay – bustling with activity and evening entertainment. In Marylebone, a good option is **Durrants**, a luxurious yet intimate family-run Georgian terrace hotel. Notting Hill offers even more stylish options: **Guesthouse West** is a boutique reinvention of the classic B&B, while the marvellously quirky **Portobello Hotel** – a longstanding favourite with musicians and celebrities *du jour* – has 24 individually designed bedrooms. In Fitzrovia, try the fashionable but as yet unpretentious **Charlotte Street Hotel**, which is perfectly located for foodie exploits. If you are looking for total grandeur and luxury, Mayfair is the only real contender, and the two best options here are **The Dorchester**, which has the ace China Tang restaurant, and **Claridge's**, where Gordon Ramsay's food can be savoured. In Chelsea, try the discreetly stylish **The Capital** or the boutique chic **myhotel Chelsea**. Covent Garden is perfect for those addicted to buzz, and the **Covent Garden Hotel** is cool and calm and close to the gourmet landmark The Ivy.

Notting Hill

Assaggi
39 Chepstow Place, W2
🚇 Notting Hill Gate
📞 020 7792 5501
✛ 7/P8

Felicitous
19 Kensington Park Rd, W11
🚇 Notting Hill Gate
📞 020 7234 4050
✛ 5/B9

Le Maroc
95 Golborne Rd, W10
🚇 Ladbroke Grove
📞 020 8968 8055
✛ 5/A6

Books for Cooks
4 Blenheim Crescent, W11
🚇 Notting Hill Gate
📞 020 7221 1992
booksforcooks.com
✛ 5/A8

The Grocer on Elgin
6 Elgin Crescent, W11
🚇 Notting Hill Gate
📞 020 7437 7776
thegroceron.com
✛ 9/A8

Lisboa Delicatessen
54 Golborne Rd, W10
🚇 Ladbroke Grove
📞 020 8969 1052
✛ 5/A6

Clarke's
124 Kensington Church St, W8
🚇 Notting Hill Gate
📞 020 7221 9225
sallyclarke.com
✛ 9/D10

Kensington Place
201 Kensington Church St, W8
🚇 Notting Hill Gate
📞 020 7727 3184
egami.co.uk
✛ 9/D10

Mr Christian's
11 Elgin Crescent, W11
🚇 Notting Hill Gate
📞 020 7229 0527
jeroboams.co.uk
✛ 9/A8

Battersea and Clapham

A. Dove & Son
71 Northcote Rd, SW11
🚇 Clapham South
📞 020 7223 5191
✛ Off map

I Sapori di Stefano Cavallini
146 Northcote Rd, SW11
🚇 Clapham Common
📞 020 7228 2017
✛ Off map

M. Moen & Son
24 The Pavement, SW4
🚇 Clapham Common
📞 020 7622 1624.
moen.co.uk
✛ Off map

Hamish Johnson
48 Northcote Rd, SW11
🚇 Clapham Common
📞 020 7738 0741
✛ Off map

Lighthouse Bakery
64 Northcote Rd, SW11
🚇 Clapham South
📞 020 7228 4537
lighthousebakery.co.uk
✛ Off map

Tsunami
5 Voltaire Rd, SW4
🚇 Clapham North
📞 020 7978 1610
✛ Off map

Ethnic enclaves

19 Numara Bos Cirrik
34 Stoke Newington
Rd, N16
🚉 Dalston Kingsland
☏ 020 7249 0400
⊕ Off map

Au Lac
104 Kingsland Rd, E2
⊖ Old Street
☏ 020 7033 0588
⊕ 4/Z3

Kastoori
188 Tooting Rd, SW17
⊖ Tooting Broadway
☏ 020 8767 7027.
⊕ Off map

Mangal Ocakbasi
10 Arcola St, E8
🚉 Dalston Kingsland
☏ 020 7275 8981.
mangal.com
⊕ Off map

Maroush Gardens
1 Connaught St, W2
⊖ Marble Arch
☏ 020 7262 0222
maroush.com
⊕ 6/I8

Patogh
8 Crawford Place, W1
⊖ Edgware Road
☏ 020 7262 4015
⊕ 6/I7

Radha Krishna Bhavan
86 Tooting High St, SW17
⊖ Tooting Broadway
☏ 020 8682 0969
mcdosa.com
⊕ Off map

Ranoush Juice Bar
43 Edgware Road, W2
⊖ Marble Arch
☏ 020 7723 5929
⊕ 6/I8

Sông Quê
134 Kingsland Rd, E2
⊖ Old Street
☏ 020 7613 3222.
⊕ 4/Z3

Marylebone

Biggles
66 Marylebone Lane, W1
⊖ Bond Street
☏ 020 7224 5937
ebiggles.co.uk
⊕ 6/L8

Caffé Caldesi
118 Marylebone Lane, W1
⊖ Bond Street
☏ 020 7935 1144
caffecaldesi.com
⊕ 6/L8

Le Pain Quotidien
72 Marylebone High
St, W1
⊖ Bond Street
☏ 020 7616 8036
orrery.co.uk
⊕ 6/L6

Orrery Epicerie
55-57 Marylebone High
St, W1
⊖ Baker Street
☏ 020 7616 8036
⊕ 6/L6

Patisserie Valerie
105 Marylebone High
St, W1
⊖ Marylebone
☏ 020 7935 6240
patisserie-valerie.co.uk
⊕ 6/L6

Paul
115 Marylebone High St, W1
⊖ Bond Street
☏ 020 7224 5616
paul.fr
⊕ 6/L6

Fitzrovia

Chez Gérard
8 Charlotte St, W1
⊖ Goodge Street
℃ 020 7636 4975
chezgerardcharlottest.
pm.co.uk
⊕ 7/N6

Fino
33 Charlotte St, W1
⊖ Goodge Street
℃ 020 7813 8010
⊕ 7/N6

Passione
10 Charlotte St, W1
⊖ Goodge Street
℃ 020 7636 2833
passione.co.uk
⊕ 7/N6

Pied à Terre
34 Charlotte St, W1
⊖ Goodge Street
℃ 020 7636 1178
⊕ 7/N6

Rasa Samudra
5 Charlotte St, W1
⊖ Goodge Street
℃ 020 7637 0222
⊕ 7/N6

Roka
37 Charlotte St, W1
⊖ Goodge Street
020 7580 6464
⊕ 7/N6

Exmouth Market

Ambassador Café
55 Exmouth Market, EC1
⊖ Farringdon
℃ 020 7837 0009.
theambassadorcafe.co.uk
⊕ 4/T5

Brindisa
32 Exmouth Market, EC1
⊖ Farringdon
℃ 020 7713 1666.
brindisa.com
⊕ 4/T5

Eagle
159 Farringdon Rd, EC1
⊖ Farringdon
℃ 020 7837 1353
⊕ 8/T6

Exmouth Market
Exmouth Market, EC1
⊖ Farringdon
exmouthmarket.co.uk
⊕ 4/T5

Little Bay
171 Farringdon Rd, EC1
⊖ Farringdon
℃ 020 7278 1234
little-bay.co.uk
⊕ 8/T6

Medcalf
40 Exmouth Market, EC1
⊖ Farringdon
℃ 020 7833 3533
medcalfbar.co.uk
⊕ 4/T5

Moro
34-Exmouth Market, EC1
⊖ Farringdon
℃ 020 7833 8336
moro.co.uk
⊕ 4/T5

Quality Chop House
92 Farringdon Rd, EC1
⊖ Farringdon
℃ 020 7837 5093
qualitychophouse.co.uk
⊕ 8/T6

Santore
59 Exmouth Market, EC1
⊖ Farringdon
℃ 020 7812 1488
⊕ 4/T5

Where to stay

Brown's
Albemarle St, W1
⊖ Green Park
© 020 7493 6020
brownshotel.com
⊕ 11/M10

The Capital
22 Basil St, SW3
⊖ Knightsbridge
© 020 7589 5171
capitalhotel.co.uk
⊕ 10/J13

Charlotte Street Hotel
21 Charlotte St, W1
⊖ Tottenham Court Rd
© 020 7806 2000
firmdale.com
⊕ 7/N6

Claridge's
Brook St, W1
⊖ Bond Street
© 0808 238 0245
claridges.co.uk
⊕ 6/H9

Covent Garden Hotel
10 Monmouth St, WC2
⊖ Covent Garden
© 020 7806 1000
firmdalehotels.com
⊕ 7/P8

The Dorchester
Park Lane, W1
⊖ March Arch
© 020 7629 8888
thedorchester.com
⊕ 10/L10

Durrants Hotel
George St, W1
⊖ Marble Arch
© 020 7935 8131
durrantshotel.co.uk
⊕ 6/J7

Great Eastern Hotel
Liverpool St, EC2
⊖ Liverpool Street
© 020 7618 5000
greateastern.hyatt.com
⊕ 8/Y7

Guesthouse West
163 Westbourne Grove,
W11
⊖ Notting Hill Gate
© 020 7792 9800
guesthousewest.com
⊕ 5/C8

The Hempel
31 Craven Hill Gdns, W2
⊖ Lancaster Gate
© 020 7298 9000
the-hempel.co.uk
⊕ 5/F9

Myhotel Chelsea
35 Ixworth Place, SW3
⊖ South Kensington
© 08707 544 447
myhotels.com
⊕ 14/H15

Portobello Hotel
22 Stanley Gdns, W11
⊖ Notting Hill Gate
© 020 7727 2777
portobello-hotel.co.uk
⊕ 5/B9

03

Weardowney Guesthouse
9a Ashbridge St, NW8
⊖ Marylebone
© 020 7725 9694
weardowney.com
⊕ 2/H5

The Zetter
86 Clerkenwell Rd, EC1
⊖ Farringdon
© 020 7324 4444
thezetter.com
⊕ 8/T6

See page 9 to scan the directory

FINE FOODS
AND CONDIMENTS

Fortnum & Mason
181 Piccadilly, W1

Previous page: Rococo
321 King's Road, SW3

Britain has a rich history of making biscuits, confectionary, jams and relishes. Many of its traditional preserves have resulted from Britain's contact, through trade and empire, with other nations. Marmalade, for instance, was first made in the late 17th century as a way of preserving the bitter oranges imported from Seville. The word 'marmalade' actually dates back much further, but previously was applied to any fruit preserved in sugar. Chutneys, relishes, gingerbread and other spiced produce made their appearance in the 19th century, after traders began importing pickles and spices from India.

04

Best of British

It was in the 19th century, too, that food manufacturing took off, leading to the emergence of many renowned British brands. The world-famous Coleman's mustard, available at **Partridges,** was first produced in 1814, when Jeremiah Coleman established his factory in Norwich. The spiced anchovy paste Patum Peperium was created by John Osborn in 1828 and became a sophisticated snack for the upper classes, hence its nickname Gentleman's Relish; it can be found at **MacFarlane's** or **Fortnum & Mason** (see Grand Food Halls overleaf).

A. Gold
42 Brushfield Street, E1

Certain parts of Britain have become indelibly associated with the foods they produce: the Yorkshire town of Harrogate is famous for its toffee (and its tea); Dundee in Scotland has a fruit cake named after it; and Worcestershire is known for its sauce although, as with many supposedly British goods, this one's origins actually lie in India.

Not all of this heritage has survived, of course, but a significant part of it can be found in London's department stores, food halls and specialist shops. Spurred on by Britain's culinary revival, many of these are now full of British products. A good place to start is **A. Gold** in Spitalfields. The owners of this small but beautiful shop, Ian and Safia Thomas, have scoured the country for the best producers, and the result is an amazing collection of delicious goods. Look for the superb jams, chutneys and pickles made by Yorkshire brand Rosebud Preserves; the nostalgia-inducing sweets in tall jars (cola bottles, pear drops, lemon bonbons); and the unusual selection of fruit juices and cordials, especially those made by Duskin, as well as British alcoholic drinks such as mead and the fermented pear juice known as perry.

04

Grand food halls

For a one-stop food shopping experience in London, **Harrods** remains a winner: in its vast food hall on the ground floor, you'll find more than 150 teas, and endless shelves of jams and relishes. These days, Harrods is facing tough competition from **Fortnum & Mason**. This venerable Piccadilly institution, established in 1707, has emerged revitalised from its 2007 refurbishment. The red carpets may still be in place at least on some floors, but with the new white-washed walls and state-of-the-art shelving, the shop now has a lighter, more streamlined feel. And its dedication to stocking the full gamut of British jams, relishes and other condiments is remarkable. The marmalade counter stocks 25 varieties and the biscuit selection

Flâneur
41 Farringdon Road, EC1

includes near-forgotten regional specialities such as Lancashire flips, Yorkshire parkin and fruit Shrewsbury. While the majority of goods are Fortnum's own, there's a liberal sprinkling of other brands, including Jules & Sharpie's enticing range of bottled jellies, and Barbieri's Mostarda di Voghera (Italian fruit mustards).

Two other food halls worth visiting are **Villandry** on Great Portland Street and **Flâneur** on Farringdon Road, both of which stock a large range of innovative artisanal products. They have a French and Italian bias, but sell foods from other European countries, too, including Britain. Villandry's range of French butter biscuits is particularly impressive; at Flâneur you will find unusual dips and bottled sauces. The store also has an excellent selection of fresh foods as well as custom prepared hampers.

Traditional Italian

London has been a destination for Italian immigrants ever since the late 19th century, and they brought with them a lively culture of food counters, coffee bars and ice cream parlours. Long before most Brits knew the difference between mozzarella and mortadella, there were Italian grocers in central parts of town, such as Soho, Clerkenwell and Farringdon, selling everything from artichoke hearts to panettone. Many of the oldest stores still survive, **L. Terroni & Sons** on the Clerkenwell Road, for instance, dates back to 1878.

04

The real backbone of this tradition is **Lina Stores** in Soho. A family-run delicatessen, established in the 1930s, it retains its original pistachio façade and traditional layout, with a single counter running through the shop and walls stacked high with goods, including risotto rices, tinned clams, sauces, dried mushrooms and truffles. Owner Tony Filippi makes fresh spaghetti, tagliatelli and ravioli daily in the backroom, as well as his own garlic and wine sausages. The shop has long been a favourite with such prominent British foodies as Jamie Oliver and Nigella Lawson.

A world of chocolate

British artisan chocolate-making has taken off since 2000, and London is now home to some truly innovative chocolate makers. Few are more refined than **L'Artisan du Chocolat** in Knightsbridge. The owner, ex-chef Gerard Coleman, is Britain's only producer to use his own dark and milk chocolate, which is manufactured at his Kent workshop. His ultra-fresh chocolates include salted caramel truffles. **Rococo**, on the King's Road, sells excellent truffles and fruit creams, along with chocolate bars with unusual ingredients such as tobacco, orange and geranium, and basil and Persian lime.

Another cutting-edge chocolatier is **Paul A. Young** in Islington. Young makes his chocolates daily in the kitchen below his shop, and is justifiably proud of such award-winning ideas as sea-salted caramel and raspberry ganache. More traditional chocolates, including handmade Yorkshire truffles, are available at **The Chocolate Society** in Belgravia.

Rococo
321 King's Road, SW3

New Italian and southern European

In the last decade or so, a modern reinvention of the classic Italian food shop has swept through town in the form of **Carluccio's**. Starting from its original site on Neal Street, Covent Garden, the company has expanded at breakneck pace, and today has nearly 20 outlets spread out across the capital. Ingeniously, each combines three functions in one: coffee shop, simple Italian restaurant and delicatessen. Look out for the unusual selection of dried pastas, including *conchiglioni* (big shells) and *bretelloni* (long crimped ribbons), and the delicious *cantucci* dry biscuits, which are the perfect dipping companion to Carluccio's *vin santo* (sweet wine).

04

For French packaged goods, try **Comptoir Gascon** in Farringdon, a classy shop that does superb foie gras, terrines and cassoulets from southwest France. Fine Spanish goods, including smoked paprika, paella rice and chocolate powder, can be found at **Brindisa** in Exmouth Market and at **R. Garcia & Sons**.

Asian, Indian and Middle Eastern

London's ethnic diversity also means that it has a range of Asian, Indian and Middle Eastern shops. **Loon Fung** in Chinatown stocks authentic Chinese vegetables, cookware and sauces (look for the Lee Kum Kee range); an even better selection is available at **Wing Yip**

Konditor & Cook
22 Cornwall Road, SE1

on Edgware Road. **Sri Thai** in Shepherd's Bush is the best place for Thai ingredients. Indian spices, vegetables and cooking equipment can be found at **Taj Stores** on Brick Lane, while there look out for Rajah's spices and pickles).

Two shops on Kensington High Street are excellent sources of Iranian food: **Reza Patisserie** sells wonderful freshly baked pastries, while **Super Bahar** next door stocks Iranian staples such as pickled garlic cloves and scented waters, caskets of saffron and, notoriously, London's best selection of wholesale-priced Iranian caviar. Bring cash, because credit cards aren't accepted.

Cookies, confectionary and spices

Divinely rich cakes and handmade biscuits and cookies are available from two bakery and cake shops, **Konditor & Cook** and **Baker & Spice**, both of which have several branches. Look out, too, for biscuits made by Popina, a London-based company that does unusual combinations such as white chocolate and fig. For an unusual confectionary gift, try **Minamoto Kitchoan** on Piccadilly, an exquisite shop selling Japanese sweets made from unusual ingredients such as aduki bean paste, chestnuts and rice flour pastry.

04

All the food halls mentioned above stock good ranges of honey, but if you want something special try the **Hive Honey Shop** in Battersea. Not only does it have a large collection of single-flower honeys produced from the owner's own hives – as well as other honey-based products such as chocolates, relishes, mustards and meads – but at the back of the shop there is a glass-fronted working hive containing 20,000 bees.

A wonderful place for spices is **The Spice Shop** off Portobello Road. This tiny store sells hundreds of different spices and spice mixtures sourced from around the world by owner Birgit Erath. The spices come in attractive yellow tins, matching the outside of the store.

Best of British

A. Gold
42 Brushfield St, E1
⊖ Liverpool Street
© 020 7247 2487
agold.co.uk
⊕ 8/Z7

Bayley & Sage
60 High St, SW19
⊖ Wimbledon
© 020 8946 9904
bayley-sage.co.uk
⊕ Off map

Bluebird Epicerie
350 Kings Rd, SW3
⊖ Sloane Square
© 020 7559 1000
danddlondon.com
⊕ 14/H17

Food Hall
374 Old St, EC1
⊖ Old Street
© 020 7729 6005
⊕ 4/X5

Gusto & Relish
56 White Hart Lane, SW13
⊖ Kew Gardens
© 020 8878 2005
⊕ Off map

MacFarlane's
48 Abbeville Rd, SW4
⊖ Clapham South
© 020 8673 5373
⊕ Off map

Partridges
2 Duke of York Square, SW
⊖ Sloane Square
© 020 7730 0651
partridges.co.uk
⊕ 14/J15

Paul Rothe & Son
35 Marylebone Lane, W
⊖ Bond Street
© 020 7935 6783
⊕ 6/L8

Twinings
216 The Strand, WC2
⊖ Temple
© 020 7353 3511
twinings.co.uk
⊕ 11/Q10

Grand food halls

Flâneur
41 Farringdon Rd, EC1
⊖ Farringdon
© 020 7404 4422
flaneur.com
⊕ 8/T6

Fortnum & Mason
181 Piccadilly, W1
⊖ Green Park
© 020 7734 8040
fortnumandmason.co.uk
⊕ 11/M11

Harrods
87 Brompton Rd, SW1
⊖ Knightsbridge
© 020 7730 1234
harrods.com
⊕ 10/I13

Harvey Nichols
109 Knightsbridge, SW1
⊖ Knightsbridge
© 020 7235 5000
harveynichols.com
⊕ 10/J12

Selfridges
400 Oxford St, W1
⊖ Bond Street
© 0800 123 4000
selfridges.co.uk
⊕ 6/K8

Villandry
170 Great Portland St, W
⊖ Great Portland Street
© 020 7631 3131
villandry.com
⊕ 6/M6

Traditional Italian

Gastronomia Italia
8 Upper Tachbrook St,
SW1
⊖ Victoria
℃ 020 7834 2767
⊕ 14/N15

Gastronomica
2 Bedale St, SE1
⊖ London Bridge
℃ 020 7407 4488
⊕ 12/X11

G. Gazzano & Sons
169 Farringdon Rd, EC1
⊖ Farringdon
℃ 020 7837 1586
⊕ 8/T6

I. Camisa & Sons
61 Old Compton St, W1
⊖ Piccadilly Circus
℃ 020 7437 7610
⊕ 7/P9

**I Sapori di Stefano
Cavallini**
146 Northcote Rd, SW11
⊖ Clapham South
℃ 020 7228 2017
⊕ Off map

L. Terroni & Sons
138 Fulham Rd, SW10
⊖ Fulham Broadway
℃ 020 7352 7739
⊕ 13/F17

Lina Stores
18 Brewer St, W1
⊖ Piccadilly Circus
℃ 020 7437 6482
⊕ 7/O9

Luigi's Delicatessen
349 Fulham Rd, SW10
⊖ Fulham Broadway
℃ 020 7352 7739
⊕ 13/F17

Olga Stores
30 Penton St, N1
⊖ Angel
℃ 020 7837 5467
⊕ 3/S3

04

New Italian and southern European

Brindisa
32 Exmouth Market, EC1
⊖ Farringdon
℃ 020 7713 1666
brindisa.com
⊕ 4/T5

Carluccio's
St Christopher's Place, W1
⊖ Bond Street
℃ 020 7935 5927
carluccios.com
⊕ 6/L8

Comptoir Gascon
63 Charterhouse St, EC1
⊖ Farringdon
℃ 020 7608 0851
clubgascon.com
⊕ 8/T7

R. Garcia & Sons
248 Portobello Rd, W11
⊖ Ladbroke Grove
℃ 020 7221 6119
⊕ 5/A6

T. Adamou & Sons
124 Chiswick High Rd, W4
⊖ Turnham Green
℃ 020 8994 0752
⊕ Off map

Truc Vert
42 North Audley St, W1
⊖ Bond Street
℃ 020 7941 9988
trucvert.co.uk
⊕ 6/K9

Asian, Indian and Middle Eastern

Loon Fung
42 Gerrard St, W1
⊖ Leicester Square
☎ 020 7437 7332
loonfung.co.uk
⊕ 7/P9

Sri Thai
56 Shepherd's Bush Rd, W6
⊖ Goldhawk Road
☎ 020 7602 0621
⊕ Off map

Talad Thai
326 Upper Richmond Rd
SW15
⊖ East Putney
☎ 020 8789 8084
⊕ Off map

Patel Brothers
187 Upper Tooting Rd,
SW17
⊖ Tooting Broadway
☎ 020 8762 2792
⊕ Off map

Super Bahar
349a Kensington High
St, W8
⊖ Kensington Olympia
☎ 020 7603 5083
⊕ 9/B13

Tawana
18 Chepstow Rd, W2
⊖ Westbourne Park
☎ 020 7221 6316
tawana.co.uk
⊕ 5/C7

Reza Pâtisserie
345 Kensington High St, W8
⊖ Kensington Olympia
☎ 020 7603 0924
⊕ 9/B13

Taj Stores
112 Brick Lane, E1
⊖ Liverpool Street
☎ 020 7377 0061
tajstores.co.uk
⊕ 8/Z6

Wing Yip
395 Edgware Rd, NW2
⊖ Brent Cross
☎ 020 8450 0422
wingyip.com
⊕ 6/I7

Coffee and tea

Algerian Coffee Stores
52 Old Compton St, W1
⊖ Leicester Square
☎ 020 7437 2480
algcoffee.co.uk
⊕ 7/P9

Monmouth Coffee Co.
27 Monmouth St, WC2
⊖ Covent Garden
☎ 020 737 93 516
monmouthcoffee.co.uk
⊕ 7/P8

Higgins
79 Duke St, W1
⊖ Bond Street
☎ 020 7629 3913
hrhiggins.co.uk
⊕ 6/L8

Drury Tea & Coffee Co.
3 New Row, WC2
⊖ Leicester Square
☎ 020 7836 1960
druryuk.com
⊕ 7/P9

Postcard Teas
9 Dering St, W1
⊖ Bond Street
☎ 020 7629 3654
postcardteas.com
⊕ 6/M8

Caffé Vergnano
62 Charing Cross Rd,
WC2
⊖ Leicester Square
☎ 020 7240 3512
caffeevergnano.com
⊕ 7/P8

A world of chocolate

Charbonnel et Walker
28 The Royal Arcade,
Old Bond St, W1
⊖ Green Park
© 020 7491 0939
charbonnel.co.uk
⊕ 11/N10

The Chocolate Society
36 Elizabeth St, SW1
⊖ Victoria
© 020 7259 9222
chocolate.co.uk
⊕ 10/L14

Choccywoccydoodah
47 Harrowby St, W1
⊖ Edgware Rd
© 020 7724 5465
choccywoccydoodah.com
⊕ 6/I7

La Maison du Chocolat
45-46 Piccadilly, W1
⊖ Piccadilly
© 020 7287 8500
lamaisonduchocolat.co.uk
⊕ 11/M11

L'Artisan du Chocolat
89 Lower Sloane St, SW1
⊖ Sloane Square
© 020 7824 8365
artisanduchocolat.com
⊕ 14/K15

Melt
59 Ledbury Rd, W11
⊖ Notting Hill
© 020 7727 50 30
meltchocolates.com
⊕ 5/C8

Montezuma's
51 Brushfield St, E1
⊖ Liverpool Street
© 020 7539 9208
montezumas.co.uk
⊕ 8/Z7

Paul A. Young
33 Camden Passage, N1
⊖ Angel
© 020 7424 5750
payoung.net
⊕ 4/U2

Rococo
321 King's Rd, SW3
⊖ Sloane Square
© 020 7352 5857
rocacochocolates.com
⊕ 14/H17

04

Cookies, confectionary and spices

Baker & Spice
47 Denyer St, SW3
⊖ South Kensington
© 020 7589 4734
bakerandspice.co.uk
⊕ 10/I14

The Hive Honey Shop
93 Northcote Rd, SW11
≈ Clapham Junction
© 020 7924 6233
thehivehoneyshop.co.uk
⊕ Off map

Konditor & Cook
22 Cornwall Rd, SE1
⊖ Waterloo
© 020 7261 0456
konditorandcook.com
⊕ 11/S11

Minamoto Kitchoan
44 Piccadilly, W1
⊖ Piccadilly Circus
© 020 7437 3135
kitchoan.com
⊕ 11/M11

Treacle
110 Columbia Rd, E2
⊖ Shoreditch
© 020 7729 5657
treacleworld.com
⊕ 4/Z4

The Spice Shop
1 Blenheim Crescent, W11
⊖ Notting Hill Gate
© 020 7221 4448
thespiceshop.co.uk
⊕ 5/A8

See page 9
to scan the
directory

FRESH PICKS AND
FARMERS MARKETS

Paxton & Whitfield
93 Jermyn Street, SW1

Previous page: Clarke's
124 Kensington Church Street, W8

I t is no exaggeration to say that there has been a produce revolution in Britain during the last ten years. Two or three decades ago, few in Britain gave much thought to where food came from, but these days more and more people care passionately about the origins and the taste of the food they eat. They want to know where it was made, whether it was produced ethically, whether it contains chemicals, and if so, which ones. Not surprisingly, this has led to a big improvement in what is available.

05

Quality revolution

The impact of this produce revolution has been especially pronounced in London. Where the capital once had only a handful of good food shops, it now has hundreds. Where there were only a few often shabby food markets, now there is a lively farmers market scene. Organic produce is a good example of how things have changed. Once regarded as being mainly for hippies, organic food is mainstream these days. All major supermarkets have substantial – and generally high quality – organic sections, and most of the places discussed in this chapter sell partly or mainly organic products.

Organic research

Britain has several organic research institutions, which monitor organic standards and provide information about organic foods and producers. These include **Garden Organic**, the **Elm Farm Research Centre** and the **Soil Association**. Look out in particular for foods bearing the Soil Association logo: its organic standard is the most rigorous in Europe. The Prince of Wales has his own organic label, **Duchy Originals**, which produces an excellent range of meats, jams and biscuits; he has also published a book, *The Elements of Organic Gardening: Highgrove, Clarence House, Birkhall.*

Planet Organic
42 Westbourne Grove, W2

Organic shops

There are a number of specialist organic supermarkets and stores around town. Until recently, the two biggest chains were **Planet Organic** and **Fresh & Wild**. Both sell a wide range of goods – everything from fruit and vegetables to pasta and tofu, and both have eating-in areas. In summer 2007, however, a far bigger player arrived on the scene: the American organic supermarket giant **Whole Foods Market,** which also owns Fresh & Wild, opened its first UK store on Kensington High Street. Offering a mammoth selection of organic goods, the chain may transform organic shopping in Britain. At the opposite end of the scale, the organic specialist **Bumblebee Natural Foods** is worth visiting in Kentish Town. Spread across three premises, it offers dried goods, fruit and vegetables, herbs and spices and wines, and also does home deliveries and a vegetable box scheme *(see Chapter Ten)*.

05

A culinary magnet

Bustling **Borough Market** is justifiably regarded as London's premier food shopping destination. Situated under the railway arches on the South Bank near London Bridge station, it is home to more than 100 stalls and shops selling both British produce and top quality food from around the world. The market is open on Thursdays (11am to 5pm), Fridays (noon to 6pm) and

Borough Market
Stoney Street, SE1

Saturdays (9am to 4pm). If you go on Saturday, arrive as early as possible, as it gets very crowded by mid-morning. Everything here is of excellent quality, and is often organic, but even so there are a few stand-outs. **Northfield Farm** does excellent, well-hung beef and lamb from rare animal breeds. **Booths** sells an exotic range of vegetables and also has a superb wild mushroom selection. **Gastronomica** and **Sardinia Organic** both sell a delicious array of Italian produce. And **Flour Power City** sells amazing fresh, artisanal breads and cakes.

Farmers markets

05

Borough Market faces increasingly stiff competition from the farmers markets springing up across the city. London's first farmers market opened in Islington in 1999; today there are more than 20. The idea behind them is that all the food should come from within 100 miles of the market and should be sold by the producers themselves. In fact, not all the so-called farmers markets in town meet these criteria. However, even those that don't (see www.lfm.org.uk) such as **Broadway Market** and **Exmouth Market** are often worth a visit. Of the bona fide farmers markets, particularly recommended are **Marylebone**, **Notting Hill** and **Blackheath**: Notting Hill, for the

Ginger Pig
8-10 Moxon Street, W1

excellent fish stall, Blackheath for first-class meat, cheese and bread, and Marylebone because you can combine a trip with stops at the excellent shops and cafés around Marylebone High Street. One thing to remember is that most farmers markets are only open one day a week, and then often for just a few hours, so it is worth checking times carefully before making a trip.

Specialist butchers

Meat has long been a cornerstone of the British diet and people have really started to take great interest in its quality. The upshot is a dramatic improvement in the range and quality of meat available. Meat is good at all the markets discussed above, as well as at Harrods, Selfridges and Harvey Nichols. But there are also some superb specialist butchers. **C. Lidgate** in Holland Park is justifiably renowned for its naturally reared, mainly organic beef and lamb – much of which comes from Prince Charles' farm at Highgrove – and for its home-made pies and prepared dishes.

The Ginger Pig in Marylebone (there is also a stall at Borough Market) sells 100% organic pork and beef, almost all of which comes from the owners' farm in north Yorkshire, not to mention the best sausages in London. **Butcher & Edmonds**, in Smithfield Meat Market, offers customers three-week-hung Scotch beef and a wide selection of seasonal game including woodcock, plover and snipe, as well as an expansive variety of venisons.

Kingsland, on Portobello Road, a genuine old-world family run establishment is renowned for rare breeds such as Middle White pigs and Ayrshire cattle, and is the place to go for juicy, homemade meat pies and unusual meats such as crocodile.

05

Steve Hatt
88-90 Essex Road, N1

Fishmongers

What's true for meat is true for fish: markets and food halls are good places, but there are also some top notch fishmongers. **James Knight** on Notting Hill Gate has a wonderful-looking selection of impeccably fresh produce; the venerable **H.S. Linwood & Sons** in the City has an extensive range of shellfish: both places offer free home delivery. **Steve Hatt**, in Islington, has long been a favourite with north Londoners – justifiably so, since the fish is superb. Bring cash, as the shop doesn't accept credit cards. For more exotic catches, such as octopus or kingfish, a good place is **Golborne Fisheries** near Ladbroke Grove: most of its stock comes from abroad, and it is still immaculately fresh. Also check out for **FishWorks**, an upmarket chain of fishmongers and fish restaurants with stores around London.

05

Greengrocers

Specialist greengrocers in London tend to be Greek-Cypriot. Two that are particularly worth a visit are **Andreas Georghiou & Co** in Chiswick and **Michanicou Brothers** in Holland Park: both sell a spectacular selection of fresh produce from around the world. The grand food halls of Harrods, Harvey Nichols and Selfridges are other places to find stunning displays of exotic fruit and vegetables.

Labelling laws

All packaged food sold in Britain is required by law to have a label stating the ingredients, in descending order of quantity. Bear in mind that a label that identifies a product as British is no guarantee that it actually originated there: food not grown in Britain but packed there can still be labelled British.

Buying organic is the best way of guaranteeing that pesticides and other chemicals have been kept to a minimum for fruit and vegetables and that animals have been reared humanely.

Of the various organic certification bodies in Britain, the **Soil Association** is the UK's largest organics body and has the most stringent standards in Europe. Be wary of non-organic markings on meat, such as Red Tractor, Farm Assured and British Quality. Although these labels signify that producers have complied with basic welfare requirements, intensive production is still allowed. When buying fresh fish, look out for the mark of the **Marine Stewardship Council** (MSC), which guarantees that the catch comes from a sustainable source. The Fairtrade logo guarantees that the producer has received a fair price.

Cheesemongers

The cheesemaking tradition has always been strong in Britain, and the produce revolution has helped to raise quality and demand for locally produced farm cheeses. The ideal place to start investigating is **Neal's Yard Dairy**. Selling mainly British and Irish cheese in its stores in Covent Garden and Borough Market, this dairy is a delight. The cheese is beautifully displayed, and knowledgeable staff happily provide free samples to help you decide. Sample classics such as Montgomery's Cheddar, ultra-smooth crème fraîche, homemade yoghurt and crusty bread.

05

Another good place for British cheeses is **Paxton & Whitfield**, established 1797 and frequented by Winston Churchill in the past. The dinner party selection of British Cheese Festival winners is, naturally, a winner, but also look for quirkly named Ticklemans hard goat's cheese and Mrs Kirkham's sublime Lancashire. French cheeses are also available and for a seriously Gallic cheese experience, try **La Fromagerie**, which has branches in both Marylebone and Highbury. Alongside the magnificent selection of Continental regional cheeses, it also has a small but delicious range of charcuterie and bottled products.

Organic shops

**Bumblebee
Natural Foods**
30 Brecknock Rd, N7
⊖ Kentish Town
℡ 020 7607 1936
bumblebee.co.uk
⊕ Off map

Fresh & Wild
49 Parkway, NW1
⊖ Mornington Crescent
℡ 020 7428 7575
freshandwild.com
⊕ 2/M1

Luscious Organic
240 Kensington High St, W8
⊖ High Street Kensington
℡ 020 7371 6987
⊕ 9/B13

The Organic Grocer
17 Clifton Rd, W9
⊖ Warwick Avenue
℡ 020 7286 1400
⊕ 1/F5

Planet Organic
42 Westbourne Grove, W2
⊖ Bayswater
℡ 020 7727 2227
planetorganic.com
⊕ 5/C8

Whole Foods Market
The Barkers Centre,
⊖ High Street Kensington, W8
wholefoodsmarket.com/uk
⊕ 9/B13

Organic research

Duchy Originals
℡ 020 8831 6800
duchyoriginals.com

**Elm Farm
Research Centre**
℡ 0148 865 8298
efrc.com

Garden Organic
℡ 0247 630 3517
gardenorganic.org.uk

Soil Association
℡ 0117 314 5000
soilassociation.org

Farmers markets

Blackheath Market
2 Blackheath Village, SE3
🚉 Blackheath
📞 020 7833 0338
Open Sunday
lfm.org.uk/black.asp
⊕ Off map

Borough Market
Stoney St, SE1
🚇 London Bridge
📞 020 7407 1002
Open: Thurs, Fri, Sat
boroughmarket.org.uk
⊕ 12/W11

Broadway Market
London Fields, E8
🚇 Bethnal Green
📞 0770 931 1869
Open Saturday
broadwaymarket.com
⊕ Off map

Marylebone Farmers Market
Cramer Street
Car Park, W1
🚇 Baker Street
Open Sunday
lfm.org.uk/mary.asp
⊕ 6/K7

Notting Hill Farmers Market
Off Kensington Pl, W8
🚇 Notting Hill Gate
Open Saturday
lfm.org.uk/nott.asp
⊕ 9/C10

Pimlico Road Farmers Market
Orange Square, corner of
Pimlico Rd & Ebury St
🚇 Sloane Square
📞 020 7833 0338
Open Saturday
lfm.org.uk/pimlico
⊕ 2/K5

05

Butchers

Allen
117 Mount St, W1
🚇 Green Park
📞 020 7499 5831
⊕ 10/K10

Butcher & Edmonds
6 Central Markets,
Smithfield, EC1
🚇 Farringdon
📞 020 7329 7388
⊕ 8/U7

C. Lidgate
110 Holland Park
Avenue, W11
🚇 Holland Park
📞 020 7727 8243
⊕ 9/B11

The Ginger Pig
8-10 Moxon St, W1
🚇 Bond Street
📞 020 7935 7788
⊕ 6/K7

Kingsland
140 Portobello Rd, W11
🚇 Notting Hill Gate
📞 020 7727 6067
⊕ 5/A6

Sheepdrove Organic Butcher
5 Clifton Rd, W9
🚇 Warwick Avenue
📞 020 7266 3838
sheepdrove.com
⊕ 1/F5

Fishmongers

FishWorks
89 Marylebone High St, W1
⊖ Baker Street
© 020 7935 9796
fishworks.co.uk
⊕ 6/L6

H.S. Linwood & Sons
6 Grand Av,
Leadenhall Market, EC3
⊖ Monument
© 020 7929 0554
⊕ 8/Y8

La Maree
76 Sloane Av, SW3
⊖ Sloane Square
© 020 7589 8067
⊕ 14/I15

Golborne Fisheries
75 Golborne Rd, W10
⊖ Ladbroke Grove
© 020 8960 3100
⊕ 5/A6

James Knight
67 Notting Hill Gate, W11
⊖ Notting Hill Gate
© 020 7221 6177
⊕ 9/C10

Steve Hatt
88-90 Essex Rd, N1
⊖ Angel
© 020 7226 3963
⊕ 4/U1

Greengrocers

Andreas Georghiou & Co
35 Turnham Green
Terrace, W4
⊖ Turnham Green
© 020 8995 0140
andreasveg.co.uk
⊕ Off map

Fry's of Chelsea
14 Cale Street, SW3
⊖ South Kensington
© 020 7589 0342
⊕ 14/H15

Michanicou Brothers
2 Clarendon Rd, W11
⊖ Holland Park
© 020 7727 5191
⊕ 9/A10

F. C. Jones
764 Fulham Rd, SW6
⊖ Parsons Green or
Putney Bridge
© 020 7736 1643
⊕ 13/F17

Hyams & Cockerton
41 Southville, SW8
⊖ Stockwell
© 020 7622 1167
⊕ Off map

Taj Stores
112 Brick Lane, E1
⊖ Aldgate East
© 020 7377 0061
⊕ 8/Z6

Cheesemongers

Bloomsbury Cheeses
61b Judd St, WC1
⊖ Russell Square
ⓒ 020 7387 7645
✛ 3/Q4

La Fromagerie
2-4 Moxon St, W1
⊖ Baker Street
ⓒ 020 7935 0341
lafromagerie.co.com
✛ 6/K7

Paxton & Whitfield
93 Jermyn St, SW1
⊖ Piccadilly Circus
ⓒ 020 7930 0259
paxtonandwhitfield.co.uk
✛ 11/N10

Hamish Johnson
48 Northcote Rd, SW11
≋ Clapham Junction
ⓒ 020 7738 0741
hamishjohnson.com
✛ Off map

Neal's Yard Dairy
17 Shorts Gardens, WC2
⊖ Covent Garden
ⓒ 020 7240 5700
nealsyarddairy.co.uk
✛ 7/Q8

Rippon Cheese Stores
26 Upper Tachbrook St,
SW1
⊖ Pimlico or Victoria
ⓒ 020 7931 0628
✛ 14/M14

05

Bakeries

De Gustibus
53-55 Carter Lane, EC4
⊖ St Paul's
ⓒ 020 7236 0056
degustibus.co.uk
✛ 8/U9

Maison Brillant
56 Upper Ground, SE1
⊖ Blackfriars
ⓒ 020 7928 8158
maisonbrillant.com
✛ 11/S11

Poilâne
46 Elizabeth St, SW1
⊖ Sloane Square
ⓒ 020 7808 4910
poilane.fr
✛ 10/L14

Euphorium Bakery
202 Upper St, N1
⊖ Angel
ⓒ 020 7704 6905
✛ 4/T2

Neal's Yard Bakery
6 Neal's Yard, WC2
⊖ Covent Garden
ⓒ 020 7836 5199
nealsyardbakery.co.uk
✛ 7/P8

See page 9
to scan the
directory

THE FAST TRACK
TO FINE WINES

Corney & Barrow
194 Kensington Park Road, W11

Previous page: Berry Bros & Rudd
3 St James's Street, SW1

Britain has always had a rather complicated relationship with wine. While its own wines have often been a laughing stock, the British upper classes have long enjoyed a reputation as discerning wine drinkers. The ability to tell the difference between a Burgundy and a claret was considered the mark of a gentleman, in much the same way that being able to consume large quantities of beer was the mark of someone from the lower orders.

This picture has been altered by two developments. First, British wine is no longer a joke; and second, wine-drinking has lost many of its elitist connotations. People from all levels of society are happy to drink wine these days, and as a result, the country's wine market has exploded; sales have gone up by 25%, and by 2010 the UK is expected to spend more on wine than any other country in Europe.

06

Expert guidance

All this has had an enormous impact on London's wine scene, resulting in a bewilderingly complex market that combines the best of traditional oenophile culture with a brashness and exuberance more typical of the

Haynes Hanson & Clark
7 Elystan Street, SW3

New World. Today's wine buyers are confronted by so many options that most will need some kind of expert guidance. Jancis Robinson's fine wines column in the Saturday *Financial Times* is an indispensable resource, as is her website, jancisrobinson.com, while Tim Atkins's column in the *Observer* is also full of reliable advice. Perhaps the best book-length resource is Oz Clarke's *Wine Buying Guide*, which offers a comprehensive overview of the wines available to the British consumer.

Wine merchants

London's oldest wine merchant and, many would argue, still its best, is **Berry Bros & Rudd** on St James's Street. Until recently, the shop had no bottles on display; you simply sat down with the staff in one of the oak-panelled rooms, and discussed your requirements. Nowadays, a small selection of bottles from the 2,500-strong stock lines the shelves.

06

Finest reserves are kept under lock and key in their own glass cabinet – not surprising, because they include 1982 Petrus at £3,800 a bottle. At the more affordable end of the scale, there's an excellent range of mid-price Bordeaux (2002 Clos du Marquis St Julien at £26) and a selection of interesting New World wines. Lacking the old-school grandeur of Berry Bros, but still traditional, is **Corney & Barrow** in Notting Hill. A tiny

Philglas & Swiggot
21 Northcote Road, SW11

yet charming shop with dedicated staff, it stocks an impressive mix of vintage French and New World wines, with Argentinian producers such as Achaval Ferrer and Bodega Lurton to the fore. Another good choice for lovers of New World wine is **Philglas & Swiggot**, which has a large selection of classics from Australia and New Zealand, among them a 2002 Isabel Noble Sauvage New Zealand Riesling. **Haynes Hanson & Clark** in south Kensington is another excellent traditional wine merchant; it offers perhaps the most extensive selection of Burgundies in the capital.

The Sampler, opened in 2006 by former venture capitalist Jamie Hutchinson in Islington, is a refreshing contrast to traditional outlets. Eschewing their stuffiness, Hutchinson brought in sleek vending machines, an Italian-designed Enomatic system, which allows customers to purchase a rechargeable card (not unlike a London transport Oyster card) and sample the wines at their optimum temperature.

06

The 680-strong range at The Sampler is well balanced between Europe and the New World, with an excellent choice of Italian varietals; (including a 1999 Barolo Vietti at £49.99 a bottle); and a few English sparkling wines, such as Nyetimber Chardonnay. For all the quaint appeal of the long-established merchants,

The Sampler wins hands down for practicality. The wines are grouped by grape, rather than country, allowing you to make direct comparisons. And because the measures are sample size, customers can try wines they would be unlikely to purchase in bottle form, such as 2002 Château Latour. If you're looking for more than just a drink, visit **Jeroboams wine merchants** whose branches across London sell cheeses, charcuterie, oils and foie gras, along with a wide selection of wines, champagnes and spirits. Among its stock is a wide variety of English white and sparkling wines, including those produced by the celebrated Three Choirs estate in Gloucestershire. **Harvey Nichols**, **Selfridges** and **Liberty** also have good wine departments; at the bar in Harvey Nichols, you can order any of the wines in the shop with a minimal mark-up.

Around Wine, a relatively new fixture on the London scene, is the best one-stop shop for all beverage accessories. With dozens of different corkscrews and just about the entire range of Riedel glasses, as well as standalone wine cellars and cellar cooling systems, this is the perfect place to find a present for a true aficionado. Most of the merchants mentioned above have websites where you can browse and order wines for home delivery. The Berry Bros & Rudd site is particularly impressive, offering useful notes on much of its stock.

Restaurants

Hefty mark-ups on wine in London's restaurants mean that you rarely find brilliant value for money. In the past the capital's restaurants made little effort to guide their customers in choosing wine. But the situation is improving. Many of London's top restaurants now boast expansive and well chosen wine lists – **Gordon Ramsay**, **Le Gavroche** and **The Capital** stand out – and restaurants generally are becoming more wine-led *(see Wine Bars, page 107)*. With this has come a change in the status of sommeliers. The old stereotype of the haughty French sommelier is on the wane and a new breed has emerged, typified

06

Auctions and special events

If you've got the money, the knowledge and nerves of steel, check out the wine auctions at Christie's and Sotheby's, which offer the opportunity to acquire rare vintage labels. Auctions are run on a regular basis – **Sotheby's** holds about 11 annually – but the price tags may deter some: a 12-bottle case of 1978

Romanée Conti sold at **Christie's** for a record-breaking £93,500 in 2006.

Christie's also teams up with industry chronicler *Decanter* magazine every October to host the Royal Opera House Gala Wine Dinner, a ritzy event with speakers and a tasting of some of the world's best wines.

Vinoteca
7 St John Street, EC1

by youthful exuberance. Top sommeliers these days are as likely to be American or Australian as French, for example Jason McAuliffe, an Australian whose charisma helped establish the reputation of **Chez Bruce** in Wandsworth and who is now doing much the same job at the Grill Room at **The Dorchester**. Matt Skinner, also Australian, has performed a similar feat at Jamie Oliver's **Fifteen**.

Wine bars with a difference

The British once looked down on wine bars as pretentious, even slightly vulgar. No longer. London has several places that pair food with wine in a straightforward and intelligent manner. **The Bleeding Heart** in Clerkenwell has a long list of outstanding wines; these it matches with no-nonsense British food. The menu at **Vinoteca**, a wine shop and restaurant in one, carries a suggested wine pairing with each dish, and the store's stock is extensive and imaginative. The pricing is also refreshingly transparent: each bottle is labelled with the drink-in and take-away price, as well as extensive tasting notes. If you're going out for just a drink, **Gordon's Wine Bar** off the Embankment, which claims to be London's oldest wine bar, is very entertaining. The **Cork & Bottle**, a homely cellar discreetly tucked in between a sex shop and a pizza parlour near Leicester Square, has a superb 28-page wine list and excellent bar food.

06

Likewise, energetic **Smithy's Wine Bar**, on a back street in King's Cross, has an impressive selection of wines as well as real ales. **The Arches** in Hampstead is also well worth a visit for its wine list.

Wine courses and mail order clubs

Many merchants hold regular wine-tasting events and/or courses. Indeed, the capital is awash with wine education programmes. Christie's and Sotheby's both run their own, and there are plenty of other options depending on budget, interest and experience – try the **Docklands Wine School**, the **Connoisseur Wine School**, the **Institut Français** and the **London Wine Academy**. There are also excellent mail order wine clubs: some charge a joining fee, but this is often well worth paying for the bargains and the range available. **The Wine Society**, **Stone, Vine & Sun** and **Averys** are all consistently good.

Wine merchants and auctioneers

Around Wine
40 New Cavendish St, W1
⊖ Bond Street
ⓒ 020 7935 4679
aroundwine.co.uk
⊕ 6/L7

Harvey Nichols
109 Knightsbridge, SW1
⊖ Knightsbridge
ⓒ 020 7235 5000
harveynichols.com
⊕ 10/J12

Philglas & Swiggot
21 Northcote Rd, SW11
⊖ Clapham South
ⓒ 020 7924 4494
philgas-swiggot.co.uk
⊕ Off map

Berry Bros & Rudd
3 St James's St, SW1
⊖ Green Park
ⓒ 020 7396 9600
bbr.com
⊕ 11/N11

**Haynes Hanson
& Clark**
7 Elystan St, SW3
⊖ South Kensington
ⓒ 020 7584 7927
hhandc.co.uk
⊕ 14/I15

The Sampler
266 Upper St, N1
⊖ Highbury & Islington
ⓒ 020 7226 9500
thesampler.co.uk
⊕ 4/T2

Christie's
8 King St, SW1
⊖ Green Park
ⓒ 020 7839 9060
christies.com
⊕ 11/N11

Jeroboams
50 Elizabeth St, SW1
⊖ Sloane Square
ⓒ 020 7730 8108
jeroboams.co.uk
⊕ 10/L14

Selfridges
400 Oxford St, W1
⊖ Bond Street
ⓒ 0800 123 400
selfridges.com
⊕ 6/K8

Corney & Barrow
194 Kensington
Park Rd, W11
⊖ Ladbroke Grove
ⓒ 020 7221 5122
corneyandbarrow com
⊕ 5/B9

Liberty
Great Marlborough St, W1
⊖ Oxford Circus
ⓒ 020 7734 1234
liberty.co.uk
⊕ 7/N8

Sotheby's •
34 New Bond St, W1
⊖ Bond Street
ⓒ 020 7293 5000
sothebys.com
⊕ 6/M8

06

Restaurants

The Capital
22 Basil St, SW3
⊖ Knightsbridge
☏ 020 7589 5171
capitalhotel.co.uk
⊕ 10/J13

Chez Bruce
2 Bellevue Rd, SW17
⌗ Wandsworth Common
☏ 020 8672 0114
chezbruce.co.uk
⊕ Off map

The Dorchester
Park Lane, W1
⊖ Hyde Park Corner
☏ 020 7629 8888
thedorchester.com
⊕ 10/L10

Fifteen
15 Westland Pl, N1
⊖ Old Street
☏ 0871 330 1515
fifteen.net
⊕ 6/K9

Gordon Ramsay at Claridge's
Claridge's, Brook St, W1
⊖ Bond Street
☏ 020 7499 0099
gordonramsay.com
⊕ 6/L9

Le Gavroche
43 Upper Brook St, W1
⊖ Bond Street
☏ 020 74080881
le-gavroche.co.uk
⊕ 6/K9

Wine courses

Christie's Education
153 Great Titchfield St, W1
⊖ Great Portland St
christies.com/education
⊕ 6/M6

Connoisseur Wine School
10 Wedderburn Rd, NW3
⊖ Hampstead
☏ 0795 687 0772
connoisseur.org
⊕ Off map

Docklands Wine School
☏ 0779 669 0884
rawlings-and-wine.com

Institut Français
17 Queensberry Place, SW7
⊖ South Kensington
☏ 020 7073 1350
institut-francais.org.uk
⊕ 14/G14

London Wine Academy
Garden Floor, 6 Coldbath Sq, EC1
⊖ Farringdon
☏ 0870 100 0100
londonwineacademy.com
⊕ 8/U5

Sotheby's
34 New Bond St, W1
⊖ Bond Street
☏ 020 7293 5000
sothebys.com/wine
⊕ 6/M8

Wine bars with a difference

The Arches
7 Fairhazel Gardens, NW6
⊖ Swiss Cottage
☏ 020 7624 1867
⊕ Off map

Cork & Bottle
44 Cranbourn St, WC2
⊖ Leicester Square
☏ 020 7734 7807
donhewitson.com
⊕ 7/P9

The Milestone Hotel
1 Kensington Court, W8
⊖ High Street Kensington
☏ 020 7917 1000
milestonehotel.com
⊕ 9/B13

The Bleeding Heart
Bleeding Heart Yard, off
Greville St, EC1
⊖ Farringdon
☏ 020 7242 2056
bleedingheart.co.uk
⊕ 8/T7

Gordon's Wine Bar
47 Villiers St, WC2
⊖ Embankment
☏ 020 7930 1408
gordonswinebar.co.uk
⊕ 11/Q10

Smithy's Wine Bar
15 Leeke St, WC1
⊖ King's Cross
☏ 020 7278 5949
smithyslondon.com
⊕ 3/R3

Cellar Gascon
59 West Smithfield, EC1
⊖ Farringdon
☏ 020 7796 0600
⊕ 8/U7

Grill Room
The Dorchester
53 Park Lane, W1
⊖ Hyde Park Corner
☏ 020 7629 8888
thedorchester.com
⊕ 10/L10

Vinoteca
7 St John St, EC1
⊖ Farringdon
☏ 020 7253 8786
vinoteca.co.uk
⊕ 8/U6

06

Mail order clubs

Averys
☏ 08451 283 797
averys.com

Stone, Vine & Sun
☏ stonevine.co.uk

The Wine Society
☏ 0143 874 0222
thewinesociety.com

See page 9
to scan the
directory

COOKERY SCHOOLS
AND MASTER CLASSES

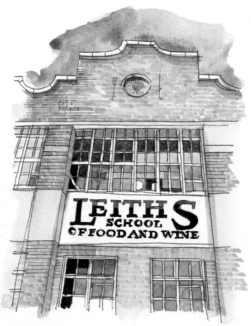

Leiths School of Food and Wine
21 St Alban's Grove, W8

Previous page: Divertimenti
33-34 Marylebone High Street, W1

A s the food in the city's restaurants has become more refined and exotic, Londoners have started thinking about developing and improving their own culinary skills. As a result, London's cookery school scene is thriving. More and more amateur cooks are discovering that hands-on tuition from a professional is often a more effective way of learning to cook than studying a recipe book or watching a TV show. True, it can be pretty expensive, but in a city like London, there is no shortage of people who can afford the fees.

It's not only specialist cookery schools that run classes, however. Specialist shops and, increasingly, restaurants are getting in on the act, too. The upshot is that there are now classes and courses catering to every culinary ability and aspiration. These range from one-off instruction in a specific skill, such as fish filleting or the fine art of knife grinding, to a comprehensive training in a particular cuisine or cooking style.

For full information on classes and course prices, check the websites at the end of this chapter.

07

The Avenue Cookery School
74 Chartfield Avenue, SW15

Cookery classes are not only a fantastic way to learn how to cook; they can be great fun as well. For many who attend them, part of their appeal is that they are a chance to meet like-minded people. Classes typically end with students sitting down together with the instructor and eating what they have cooked – and so an educative event turns into a social one. A few cookery schools have even gone as far as offering singles-only cooking classes with titles such as Cooking for Crumpet at **The Avenue Cookery School** in Putney or Flirting with Flavour at **La Cucina Caldesi**.

Before you sign up

A couple of things should be borne in mind before joining any cookery course. Although classes in restaurants may sound exciting in principle, offering the chance to work with a professional, restaurant chefs do not necessarily make the best teachers, and their kitchens are not always ideally set up for group learning. In fact, cookery classes in restaurants sometimes prove to be little more than demonstrations, and while these can be perfectly enjoyable, they are not a substitute for hands-on tuition. Therefore, before signing up for a class, check precisely what it will involve. Most classes get booked up months in advance, so plan well ahead.

07

Chocolate-making classes

Many of London's chocolatiers hold regular tastings and chocolate-making classes, providing access to an exciting world of flavour.

Bournemouth company **Chocolate Delight** runs weekly classes in London that involve tastings, truffle making and decorating. **My Chocolate** runs group workshops covering the origins of chocolate alongside fudge- and praline-making and are generally aimed at the stag or hen party crowd.

Besides its boutique retail outlet in Islington, **Paul A. Young** offers full-day chocolate classes for groups of four every Tuesday. Topics covered include how to taste, mould, roll, coat and decorate your truffles. Lunch with your fellow chocolatiers is included in the schedule.

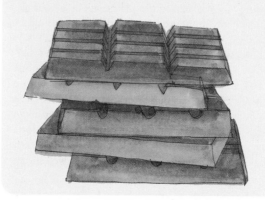

The grandest schools

The two oldest and grandest cookery schools are **Le Cordon Bleu London Culinary Arts Institute** and **Leiths School of Food and Wine**. Both are internationally famed training schools offering intensive courses for those whose ambition is to cook professionally. However, both offer short, demonstration-packed courses and classes for amateurs as well.

Le Cordon Bleu runs classes covering such subjects as boulangerie, patisserie and viennoiserie, which involve bread- and pastry-making, as well as regular evening courses introducing students to basic classical French techniques. Leiths has a range of half- and full-day workshops in subjects including knife skills, bread-making and Thai cuisine. Its popular Saturday morning sessions give pupils the chance to cook their way through a three-course menu.

Small but perfectly formed

As you would expect of such prestigious establishments, Le Cordon Bleu and Leiths provide unrivalled facilities and consistently good instruction. However, their sheer size can make attending them a slightly anonymous experience, so it is worth considering smaller London cooking schools which offer more eclectic and personal experiences. A good example is

07

La Cucina Caldesi
118 Marylebone Lane, W1

La Cucina Caldesi, a small studio kitchen in Marylebone run by Giancarlo and Katie Caldesi, whose range of courses in robust Italian cookery includes a pasta master class and a lesson in pizza making.

Another good small school is **Eat Drink Talk** in Clerkenwell. Owner Jennifer Kline gives most of the lessons herself, has travelled widely and her classes have a Pacific and pan-Asian emphasis. Many focus on a single recipe or groups of dishes: Singapore chili crab, fusion dim sung and Asian street food.

One of the best of London's small cookery schools is run from **Divertimenti**, the cookware shop. Classes are offered at both the company's locations, in Marylebone High Street and Brompton Road, and the school's reputation enables it to attract many of London's finest chefs among its tutors: Skye Gyngell of Petersham Nurseries Café, Mark Hix of The Ivy and Atul Kochhar of Benares are all regulars. Look out, too, for the dumpling master classes given by the charismatic Chinese chef and flautist Guo Yue – these are always great fun.

07

Outside and in the kitchen

Food tours in London based around prestigious food destinations, take in both the retailers and the general history of the area and typically conclude with a meal cooked from the ingredients obtained. Jun Tanaka, head chef at **Pearl Bar & Restaurant**, offers his famous Shopping with the Chef sessions costing £120, these take place infrequently, so make sure to book early.

Chef and food writer **Celia Brooks-Brown** offers regular Gastrotours around some of London's most exciting food areas, including Marylebone Village, Borough Market and Portobello. (Visit her website, www.celiabrooksbrown).

If you fancy a day out of London, and are prepared to wade in coastal estuaries, climb fruit trees and generally get your clothes dirty, **Fergus Drennan** offers foraging courses in the Kent region. (Visit his website www.wildmanwildfood.com).

A new fad has been imported from the US: food preparation kitchens. At these, clients are supervised while they assemble dishes from raw ingredients, which they take home and freeze. **Dinners-Made** opened its first branch in Richmond in 2007, and more are promised. It may be a good way of stocking up your larder, but its educational value remains doubtful.

Fish preparation schools

Londoners' new-found culinary adventurousness is reflected in the growing popularity of fish and sushi classes. The capital now has two dedicated fish cookery schools: **Billingsgate Seafood Training School** and **FishWorks Cookery School** in Richmond. The former, attached to the famous fish market, offers tuition for those looking to enter the fish trade as well as classes and demonstrations for those who simply want to learn more about cooking fish at home.

Many begin with tours of the market – an exciting experience that makes getting up early worth your while. Evening classes explore the cooking of individual fishes, such as octopus or red mullet. FishWorks offers a standard day-long course, costing £225, which covers the basics of fish buying and various simple fish dishes. Tailored classes for groups can also be arranged. The **JC Sushi Academy** on Piccadilly runs two-and-a-half hour intensive sushi-making classes costing £140, on the second Tuesday of every month; it also does daily weekday classes covering various aspects of Japanese cuisine.

07

Books for Cooks
4 Blenheim Crescent, W11

Master classes in restaurants

At the most expensive end of the scale, **Tasting Places** organizes master classes in various top London restaurants, such as Gordon Ramsay, Moro and The Capital; these normally take the form of a morning demonstration followed by lunch (the cost ranges from £140-£220). A far cheaper option, at £28 a go, are the two-hour classes at **A Table** in Richmond, which usually involve cooking a simple three-course meal.

Books for Cooks in Notting Hill offers entertaining demonstrations and classes from a wide variety of tutors in its cramped studio kitchen. **Cookery School** in Little Portland Street has six-week evening courses for both beginners and intermediate cooks, and **Underground Catering** near Liverpool Street in the City offers informal group cooking sessions in the evening for £50.

07

Specialist skills courses

The Ginger Pig butcher shop in Marylebone offers evening butchery classes, while next door **La Fromagerie** runs regular cheese tastings and hosts other food events, often in conjunction with Slow Food London. The **Japanese Knife Company** does knife-sharpening courses – which may sound unnecessary, but they are well worth it if you've invested in an expensive set of knives.

Cookery schools

The Avenue
74 Chartfield Av, SW15
🚇 East Putney
📞 020 8788 3025
theavenuecourses.co.uk
⊕ Off map

Cookery School
15B Little Portland St, W1
🚇 Oxford Circus
📞 020 7631 4590
cookeryschool.co.uk
⊕ 7/N7

Divertimenti
33 Marylebone High St, W1
🚇 Baker Street
📞 020 7935 0689
divertimenti.co.uk
⊕ 6/L6

Eat Drink Talk
Unit 102,
190 St John St, EC1
🚇 Farringdon
📞 020 7689 6693
eatdrinktalk.co.uk
⊕ 8/U6

The Kids' Cookery School
107 Gunnersbury Lane, W3
🚇 Acton Town
📞 020 8992 8882
thekidscookeryschool.co.uk
⊕ Off map

La Cucina Caldesi
118 Marylebone Lane, W1
🚇 Bond Street
📞 020 7935 1144
caldesi.com
⊕ 6/L8

Le Cordon Bleu
114 Marylebone Lane, W1
🚇 Bond Street
📞 020 7935 3503
lcblondon.com
⊕ 6/L8

Leiths School of Food
21 St Alban's Grove, W8
🚇 High Street Kensington
📞 020 7229 0177
leiths.com
⊕ 9/E13

Underground Catering
4 Eldon St, EC2
📞 020 7426 2171
🚇 Liverpool Street
underground/
cookeryschool.com
⊕ 8/X7

Master classes in restaurants

Almeida
30 Almeida St, N1
🚇 Angel
📞 020 7354 4777
almeida-restaurant.co.uk
⊕ 4/V1

Amici
35 Bellevue Rd, SW17
🚇 Tooting Bec
📞 020 8672 5888
amiciitalian.co.uk
⊕ Off map

A Table
7 Arlington Rd, Richmond
🚇 Richmond
📞 020 8940 9910
atable.info
⊕ Off map

Deya
34 Portman Square, W1
🚇 Marble Arch
📞 0845 640 8000
redletterdays.co.uk
⊕ 6/K8

Tasting Places
PO Box 38174,
W10 5ZP
📞 020 8964 5333
tastingplaces.com
⊕ Off map

Pearl Bar & Restaurant
Chancery Court Hotel,
252 High Holborn, WC1
🚇 Holborn
📞 020 7829 7000
pearl-restaurant.com
⊕ 7/S7

126

Fish preparation schools

Billingsgate Seafood
28 Billingsgate Market,
Trafalgar Way, E14
⊖ Blackwall
ⓒ 020 7517 3548
seafoodtraining.org
⊕ Off map

FishWorks
13 The Square,
Old Market, Richmond
⊖ Richmond
ⓒ 020 8948 5965
fishworks.co.uk
⊕ Off map

JC Sushi Academy
Restaurant Toku,
Japan Centre,
212 Piccadilly, W1
⊖ Piccadilly Circus
ⓒ 020 7255 8255
sushi-courses.co.uk
⊕ 10/M11

Specialist skills courses

Books for Cooks
4 Bleinheim Crescent, W11
⊖ Ladbroke Grove
ⓒ 020 7221 1992
booksforcooks.com
⊕ 5/A8

DinnersMade
106 Kew Road, Richmond
⊖ Richmond
ⓒ 020 8948 8008
dinnersmade.co.uk
⊕ Off map

Flâneur
41 Farringdon Rd, EC1
⊖ Farringdon
ⓒ 020 7404 4422
flaneur.com
⊕ 8/T6

The Ginger Pig
8 Moxon St, W1
⊖ Bond Street
ⓒ 020 7935 7788
⊕ 6/K7

**Japanese
Knife Company**
137 Belsize Rd, NW6
⊖ Kilburn Park
ⓒ 0870 240 2248
japaneseknifecompany.com
⊕ Off map

La Fromagerie
2 Moxon St, W1
⊖ Baker Street
ⓒ 020 7935 0341
lafromagerie.co.uk
⊕ 6/K7

07

Chocolate-making classes

Chocolate Delight
ⓒ 0870 770 2919
chocolatedelight.co.uk

My Chocolate
16 Baldwin Gardens, EC1
⊖ Chancery Lane
ⓒ 020 7269 5760
mychocolate.co.uk
⊕ 7/S6

Paul A. Young
33 Camden Passage, N1
⊖ Angel
ⓒ 020 7424 5750
payoung.net
⊕ 4/U2

See page 9
to scan the
directory

08

CITY SECRETS FROM
CULINARY KINGS

The Wallace Restaurant
Hertford House, Manchester Square, W1

Previous page: Inn the Park
St James's Park, SW1

I n a city as large as London, knowledge gleaned from even daily culinary coverage can go only so far. There will always be that out-of-the-way restaurant or shop that only a privileged few know about, such as the bakery around the corner that does wonderful fresh bread. Here, a number of prominent figures on London's food scene – critics, restaurateurs and master chefs share their insider knowledge. Some of their sources, also mentioned in other chapters, are easy to locate; others will require a longer train, tube or taxi ride into the outer edges of central London.

Oliver Peyton: back to basics

Oliver Peyton has been one of London's most prominent restaurateurs for more than a decade, setting up the celebrated Atlantic Bar and Grill in the 1990s and, more recently, several restaurants across the capital, including **Inn the Park** and the **Wallace Restaurant**. But the food entrepreneur and founder of Peyton and Byrne Ltd, admits to being relatively unimpressed by many of London's most prestigious eateries. "I'm bored with haute cuisine," he says, adding, "There are too many average restaurants."

08

Neal's Yard Dairy
17 Shorts Gardens, WC2

According Peyton, there's definitely a "back to basics trend" in London eating habits. His tips for such roots-related establishments are **Assaggi** in Notting Hill, "one of the few genuine Italian restaurants in London," he thinks, and **Bentley's Oyster Bar & Grill** in Piccadilly for beautiful fresh seafood. The Irish boulevardier, whose eateries include the National Gallery Dining Rooms and Café, admits to loving the glitzy **Locanda Locatelli**, but suggests eating there on a Sunday, when it's much easier to get a table.

Peyton shops at **C. Lidgate** in Holland Park, which he considers "the most sophisticated butcher in London – their steak is simply the best." For fresh pasta and other Italian goods he goes to **Lina Stores** in Soho. Peyton recommends **Marylebone Farmers Market** on a Sunday because it is not nearly as crowded as Borough Market and "much more civilised." Likewise, to avoid the crowds, preferring the **Neal's Yard Dairy** in Covent Garden rather than the branch at Borough, "although they're both great shops," he adds.

08

Peyton says, **Beigel Bake**, the 24-hour bagel shop at the top of Brick Lane, is "a wonderful gourmet experience. Bagels have to be boiled, not baked, and they do them properly there." **Divertimenti**, he adds, is "a great cookware shop" and **Books for Cooks** *the* place to buy cookbooks.

Huw Gott: offbeat gastronomy

Along with his partner, Will Beckett, Huw Gott is one of London's brightest up-and-coming restaurateurs. They own several places across the capital, including Mexican restaurant **Green & Red**, the American-style steakhouse **Hawksmoor**, and gastropub **The Marquess Tavern**.

Gott describes east London, where he lives, as "a fantastic neighbourhood for cafés and food shops," full of hidden gems. "There's a place called **Elliot's Café** on Bethnal Green Road, run by an Australian chef. It's just a café really – it does salads and simple stuff, but the food is great."

Another favourite is **Leila's** on Calvert Avenue near Shoreditch High Street. "It's a sort of delicatessen and café rolled into one with a small range of excellent stuff. It does really good Polish sausage, for example, and amazing Chelsea buns."

Close to Leila's, the winner of the Young achiever 2007 award also recommends **Rochelle School Canteen**. "You need to ring the buzzer to get in. It's a really small café-bistro in an artist's studio, which does hearty dishes such as bean and chorizo stew. It's a secret, special place run by the wife of Fergus Henderson, the chef at St John.

The food is excellent."One of his cherished all-round shopping destinations is **Broadway Market**: "Look out for the excellent cake store," he says. Gott also speaks highly of the food served at **The Regent**, a pub in Kensal Green. "It only does burgers, but they're really good ones, made of good organic beef." For its "great range of English beers and ales," the restaurateur recommends **The Arbiter**, a pub in Fulham. His tip for the best Vietnamese restaurant is **Huong-Viet**, which is part of the Vietnamese Cultural Centre on Englefield Road in Dalston. "It does really good, unpretentious food, including an interesting tofu dessert."

Celia Brooks-Brown: a chef's hidden sources

Chef Celia Brooks-Brown is certainly someone who knows about shopping and eating in London, through her experience teaching at **Divertimenti** and other cookery schools, and running food tours through the city's gourmet neighbourhoods. One of her favourite places to eat is in Green Lanes, up in Harringay. "It's a very mixed area, full of very good and cheap Cypriot and Turkish shops and restaurants. But there's this Albanian café, **Bingol**, which is open 24 hours a day and serves delicious fresh vegetable dishes," she says. "There's also an excellent grocer and bakery in that area, **Yasar Halim Turkish Food Market**."

08

The passionate cook and food writer admits that one of her favourite restaurants in London is in the unlikely location of Centre Point, just behind Tottenham Court Road tube station. "There's a Korean food shop tucked away on St Giles High Street," she says, "and if you go through it and up to the first floor you'll get to a restaurant, **Centre Point Sushi**. It does phenomenal sushi and it's really cheap, and in such a convenient location."

A treasured shopping destination for Brooks-Brown is the Chinese supermarket **Wing Yip** on the Edgware Road, near Brent Cross. It appeals not only because of its large range of ingredients, she says, but because "it's got an aisle of fantastic kitchenware, including really basic and useful things like pestle and mortars."

The veggie cookbook author of world renown also recommends **Luento Santoro**, a "fantastic chocolate boutique" in Notting Hill. When Brooks-Brown feels like avoiding meat when dining out, she goes to **The Gate** in Hammersmith.

Jay Rayner: a food critic's favourites

Readers of the Jay Rayner restaurant column in *The Observer* know him to be a voracious foodie who will travel anywhere for a good meal. But when it comes to shopping, Rayner doesn't see much need to stray beyond his own neighbourhood of south London.

"There's a butcher shop in Clapham, **M. Moen & Son**, which does fantastic meat. It's not necessarily organic, though a lot of it is. The shop is so much more than a butcher's it offers charcuterie, olives, cheeses, as well as dry store goods and vegetables. There's even a row of food books, so you can walk in, plan a dinner party, and buy everything you need right away. It's everything you want a food shop to be." Another South London favourite of Rayner's is **Continental Delicatessen**, a Portuguese delicatessen in Brixton. "It's been doing what it does for many years, but it does it really well. It's the kind of place where you can get four or five kinds of chorizo instead of just one." You'd think that as a food columnist, Rayner wouldn't need too many restaurant tips, but he confesses to reading **Dos Hermanos**, a blog about London restaurants. "It's always worth looking up," he says.

Apollonia Poilâne: a baker's half dozen

Apollonia Poilâne, owner of the famed **Poilâne** bread company on Elizabeth Street in Belgravia, took over following her parents' death in a helicopter crash at the tender age of eighteen. The young bread heiress often comes to London on business and knows the city's food scene well. "When I'm in London I always end up at **Momo** for dinner," she says. "The ambience is so funny and ridiculous, and the food is good, too."

Mr Christian's
11 Elgin Crescent, W11

Apollonia's favourite food hall is **Harvey Nichols** – she thinks the packaging and presentation is "just amazing." One of her favourite delicatessens is **Mr Christian's** in Notting Hill. "It has such a beautiful set-up, and the food is all lovely." But when she's in the area she also goes to **Tom's Delicatessen** on Westbourne Grove. "It's small but has some wonderful produce." A favourite café in the centre of town is **Fernandez and Wells** on Lexington Street, in Soho. "It's a great place to grab a snack – the Iberian ham is especially good."

Fuchsia Dunlop: Asian hot spots

Fuchsia Dunlop is one of Britain's foremost experts on Chinese food. The author of two books, *Sichuan Food* and *Revolutionary Chinese Cookbook*, she also works as a consultant for **Bar Shu**, one of London's best Chinese restaurants. She describes **See Woo Hong Supermarket** in Chinatown as her favourite place for Chinese vegetables. Living in Dalston, an area with lots of Turkish and Kurdish immigrants, Dunlop says that she buys, cooks and eats "a fair amount of Turkish food." The Chinese food connoisseur particularly recommends the **Turkish Food Centre,** which sells all kinds of Turkish and even Persian ingredients: her favourites are quinces when they are in season, baklava, Greek olives, pomegranate juice and feta. Another favourite is the **Somine** restaurant on Kingsland High Street: "Two women make *gozleme*, irresistible flatbread pancakes stuffed with spinach, potato or cheese, every morning. The soups and stews there are stupendously good value." Another of her regular haunts is the **Mangal Ocakbasi** kebab house on Arcola Street, and she is also a regular at **Sông Quê** Vietnamese: "I adore their Vietnamese pancake, grilled beef in betel leaf and rice vermicelli with grilled pork and spring rolls."

08

Oliver Peyton: back to basics
peytonandbyrne.com

Assaggi
The Chepstow,
39 Chepstow Place, W2
⊖ Notting Hill Gate
Ⓒ 020 7792 9033
⊕ 5-9/D9

C. Lidgate
110 Holland Park Av,
Holland Park, W11
⊖ Holland Park
Ⓒ 0207 727 8243
⊕ 9/A10

Locanda Locatelli
8 Seymour St, W1
⊖ Marble Arch
Ⓒ 020 7935 9088
locandalocatelli.com
⊕ 6/J8

Beigel Bake
159 Brick Lane, E1
⊖ Shoreditch
Ⓒ 020 7729 0616
⊕ 8/Z6

Divertimenti
33 Marylebone High St, W1
⊖ Baker Street
Ⓒ 020 7935 0689
divertimenti.co.uk
⊕ 6/L6

Marylebone Farmers Market
Cramer St, W1
⊖ Bond Street
Ⓒ 020 7833 0338
lfm.org.uk/mary.asp
⊕ 6/K7

Bentley's Oyster Bar & Grill
11 Swallow St, W1
⊖ Piccadilly Circus
Ⓒ 020 7734 4756
bentley.org
⊕ 11/N10

Inn the Park
St James's Park, SW1
⊖ St James's Park
Ⓒ 020 7451 9999
innthepark.com
⊕ 11/N11

Neal's Yard Dairy
17 Shorts Gardens, WC2
⊖ Covent Garden
Ⓒ 020 7240 5700
⊕ 7/Q8

Books for Cooks
4 Blenheim Crescent, W11
⊖ Ladbroke Grove
Ⓒ 020 7221 1992
booksforcooks.com
⊕ 5/A8

Lina Stores
18 Brewer St, W1
⊖ Piccadilly Circus
Ⓒ 020 7437 6482
⊕ 7/O9

Wallace Restaurant
Hertford House,
Manchester Sq, W1
⊖ Bond Street
Ⓒ 01 020 7935 0687
wallacecollection.org
⊕ 6/K7

Huw Gott: offbeat gastronomy

underdog-group.com

The Arbiter
308 North End Rd, SW6
⊖ Fulham Broadway
☏ 020 7385 8001
arbiter-pubs.co.uk
⊕ 9/A14

Hawksmoor
157 Commercial St,
Spitalfields, E1
⊖ Old Street
☏ 020 7247 7392
⊕ 8/Z6

The Regent
5 Regent St, Kensal
Green, NW10
⊖ Kensal Green
☏ 020 8969 2184
theregentkensalgreen.com
⊕ 7/N9

Broadway Market
London Fields, E8
⊖ Bethnal Green
☏ 020 7241 3494
broadwaymarket.co.uk
⊕ 4/Z5

Huong-Viet
12-14 Englefield Rd, N1
⊖ Highbury & Islington
☏ 020 7249 0877
⊕ Off map

Rochelle School Canteen
Arnold Circus, E2
⊖ Shoreditch
☏ 020 7729 5677
arnoldandhenderson.com
⊕ 4/Z5

Elliot's Café
146 Bethnal Green Rd, E2
⊖ Bethnal Green
☏ 020 7613 1691
⊕ 4/Z5

Leila's
17 Calvert Avenue, E2
⊖ Shoreditch
☏ 020 7729 9789
⊕ 4/Z5

08

Green & Red
51 Bethnal Green Rd, E1
⊖ Shoreditch
☏ 020 7749 9670
greenred.co.uk
⊕ 4/Z5

The Marquess Tavern
32 Canonbury St,
Islington, N1
⊖ Highbury & Islington
☏ 020 7354 2975
marquesstavern.co.uk
⊕ Off map

Celia Brooks-Brown: a chef's hidden sources

Centre Point Sushi
20 St Giles High St, WC2
Tottenham Court Rd
020 7836 9860
cpfs.co.uk
7/P8

The Gate
51 Queen Caroline St, W6
Hammersmith
020 8748 6932
Off map

Yasar Halim Turkish Food Market
495 Green Lanes,
Harringay, N4
Turnpike Lane
020 8340 8090
Off map

Bingol
551 Green Lanes,
Harringay, N8
Turnpike Lane
020 8340 9691
Off map

Luento Santoro
6 Lancer Square, W8
High Street Kensington
020 7795 6611
luentosantoro.com
9/D12

Wing Yip
395 Edgware Rd,
Cricklewood, NW2
Barnet
020 8450 0422
wingyip.com
6/I7

Fuchsia Dunlop: Asian hot spots

Bar Shu
28 Frith St, W1
Tottenham Court Rd
020 7287 8822
bar-shu.co.uk
7/O8

See Woo Hong Supermarket
18 Lisle St, WC2
Leicester Square
020 7439 8325
7/P9

Sông Quê
134 Kingsland Rd, E2
Old Street
020 7613 3222
4/Z3

Mangal Ocakbasi
10 Arcola St, E8
Dalston Kingsland
020 7275 8981
Off map

Somine
131 Kingsland High St, E8
Dalston Kingsland
020 7254 7384
Off map

Turkish Food Centre
89 Ridley Rd, E8
Dalston Kingsland
020 7254 6754
Off map

Jay Rayner: a food critic's favourites

Continental Delicatessen
3 Atlantic Rd, SW9
⊖ Brixton
ⓒ 020 7733 3766
⊕ Off map

Dos Hermanos
majbros-blogspot.com

M. Moen & Son
24 The Pavement, SW4
⊖ Clapham Common
ⓒ 020 7622 1624
⊕ Off map

Apollonia Poilâne: a baker's half dozen

Fernandez and Wells
43 Lexington St, W1
⊖ Piccadilly Circus
ⓒ 020 7734 1546
⊕ 7/O9

Momo
25 Heddon St, W1
⊖ Piccadilly Circus
ⓒ 020 7434 4040
momoresto.com
⊕ 7/N9

Poilâne
46 Elizabeth St, SW1
⊖ Victoria
ⓒ 020 7808 4910
poilane.fr
⊕ 10/L14

Harvey Nichols
109 Knightsbridge, SW1
⊖ Knightsbridge
ⓒ 020 7235 5000
harveynichols.com
⊕ 10/J12

Mr Christian's
11 Elgin Crescent, W11
⊖ Notting Hill Gate
ⓒ 020 229 0501
mrchristians.co.uk
⊕ 5/A8

Tom's Delicatessen
226 Westbourne Grove, W11
⊖ Notting Hill Gate
ⓒ 020 7221 8818
⊕ 5/C8

08

See page 9 to scan the directory

WEDGWOOD

THE ART OF
FINE DINING

David Mellor
4 Sloane Square, SW1

Previous page: Waterford Wedgwood
158 Regent Street, W1

With so many restaurants and cafés at their doorsteps, it is a wonder that affluent Londoners should ever want to eat at home. And yet, as the popularity of cookery classes shows *(see Chapter Seven)*, the British are increasingly donning aprons and doing the cooking themselves. In the kitchen, as in so many areas, they are torn between the traditional and the state-of-the-art, between a back-to-basics belief that less is more and an endless appetite for the latest gadget. London's department stores, specialist cookshops and design emporiums serve both extremes and everyone in between. Moreover, whereas British brands once took second place to Italian, French, Scandinavian and German products, home-grown items now stand out and British designers and manufacturers have started biting back.

Great British classics

09

Since the 1960s, the **David Mellor** shop in Sloane Square has steadfastly championed British crafts through a period of general decline. Mellor's own cutlery is world famous, his signature lines now being found in museums as well as homes.

Ceramica Blue
10 Blenheim Crescent, W11

Other distinctive products stocked there originate from small workshops around the British Isles and beyond – Dartington stoneware from Devon, basket-ware from Galloway and Great Yarmouth, bakeware from Burnley, ox-horn spoons from the Lake District, turned-wood bowls and boards from the Cotswolds, and glass from Ireland and Italy.

Many of these pieces, including wood-fired pots by Svend Bayer and John Leach, do not look out of place in the capital's art galleries, in which examples can also be found (try **Contemporary Applied Arts** or the **Contemporary Ceramics Shop** for the best hand-thrown tableware). David Mellor's collection of that most basic but essential tool, the wooden spoon, is also hard to beat. Another British design guru who has made it his business to answer food lovers' every need is Terence Conran, the man behind home-store chain **Habitat**. His Michelin Building shop in South Kensington will satisfy almost any appetite, stocking every-thing from the Oyster Glove (must-have accessory for preparing oysters at home) to daughter Sophie Conran's range of porcelain cook- and tableware, pro-duced in partnership with the Portmeirion pottery. The **Conran Shop** also has an outlet on Marylebone High Street; the store has become something of a land-mark for those who worship sleek design.

09

Cath Kidston
51 Marylebone High Street, W1

Divertimenti, just down the road, stocks a *batterie de cuisine*: choice imports such as Mauviel copper cookware and Pillivuyt porcelain from France share the shelves with the classic Milton Brook mortar and pestle, London Pottery teapots and hand-turned bowls made from salvaged British hardwoods. Downstairs, Divertimenti features Falcon's range cookers and the Rolls-Royce of the domestic kitchen, the Aga (which is showcased across the road at **Grange**).

Sixties icon **Celia Birtwell** offers a fantastically quirky and witty interiors collection from her Notting Hill Boutique. Meanwhile, **Emma Bridgewater** and **Cath Kidston** offer the prettiest tableware and tea cloths. *(See page 159 for leads to still more individual-style designers).*

Of London's department stores, **Selfridges** stands out for volume and variety. In the basement, Aga kettles compete with Alessi; Cole & Mason salt and pepper grinders go head to head with Porsche; Anolon squares up to Le Creuset; and Richardson Sheffield knives look sharp alongside Global and Sabatier (although for seriously avant-garde knives you should check out the **Japanese Knife Company**). Selfridges cutlery ranges from the colourfully quirky Sabre through modern-classic stainless steel by Robert Welch to old-school silver by Arthur Price of England and Carrs.

09

Harrods
87 Brompton Road, SW1

If heirlooms are more your thing, go for **Asprey** and **Tiffany & Co.**, whose tableware oozes rarefied, timeless elegance. And if total exclusivity is what you desire, then nothing beats a bespoke dinner service by **Thomas Goode**, whose clientele includes princes and queens as well as fashion royalty – if it was good enough for Gianni Versace why not for you.

Porcelain and glassware

Harrods dazzles with its collections of glass, covering the best of Britain and Ireland (Waterford, Dartington and William Yeoward) as well as the Continent (Baccarat, Lalique and Moser). This is also where you can peruse one of the most expansive displays of English bone china and porcelain: Wedgwood, Royal Doulton, Royal Worcester and

Spode. For English china that manages to push boundaries as well as preserving heritage, try **Bodo Sperlein** at OxoTower Wharf. **Liberty**, too, distinguishes itself by neatly merging old and new, encapsulated by Katy Pills's charming cake-stands made from vintage plates. Within the old shop's oak-lined walls, you can lay your hands on everything you might need to serve the perfect English breakfast (T.G. Green's blue-and-white Cornishware and Burleigh's flower-power sets), afternoon tea (knitted tea cosies) and evening drinks (sommelier glasses by Riedel and the most foolproof bottle-openers by L'Atelier du Vin.

Retro to contemporary design

A little off the beaten track in London's East End, **Labour and Wait** prides itself on selling "proper things" that evoke a Victorian pantry or a 1950's kitchen – buckets, brushes and examples of design heritage such as Tala's dry-weight measure. On the same street, **Ella Doran** has turned the humble placemat into a work of art. A particularly good place to consult about cutting-edge contemporary wares is the **Design Museum Shop**, where you can pick up pieces by **People Will Always Need Plates**. Items featuring London-modernist architecture such as Tom Dixon's Eco Ware cups and bowls (recyclable after around five years).

09

Mind your manners

Continental lifestyles and the fall of the family meal have taken a toll on British table manners. Or have they? It is true that many of the old rules have disappeared – no one cares any more whether you pass the port to the left or the right. But while the British may seem less formal, hidden codes remain.

Dinner party guests in London are expected to be lavish with their presents.

A good bottle of Champagne or wine is a start, supplemented by flowers and/or a fine food item. It used to be considered rude and wicked, to take too much pleasure in food. These days, though, your host might just as easily be offended if you don't show excessive appreciation. So do ask for more.

The art of conversation at London dinner parties revolves around house prices, school fees and the awfulness of the London transport system. Deviate from these at your peril.

Finally, don't outstay your welcome, and always send a card or letter of thanks.

Kitchen design

The kitchen's place at the heart of the British home is reflected in the boom in dedicated shops and show-rooms, as well as a host of competing magazines devoted to this one room. Food lovers settling into the city and looking for a new kitchen should consult **Peter Jones** in Sloane Square about fitted and free-standing designs. A similar all-round service is offered by Humpherson's at **Heal's**. For a strong emphasis on the individual, try **Box3** or **Robinson & Cornish**, which makes a point of having no set styles, colours or finishes – or price list.

For traditional Shaker style, see **Fired Earth**; for more modern purism, Germany's Poggenpohl is your best bet and can be found at **Nicholas Anthony** and other high-end showrooms around the capital. The kitchens sold by **Mark Wilkinson** are, according to chef Gary Rhodes, "Made for life." The service, too, is top notch, from the tiniest detail to providing a mobile kitchen so you can carry on cooking through the installation. You can also have fun sourcing individual pieces for a freestanding stove at **Retrouvius**, **Holloways of Ludlow** and the excellent antiques stores around Portobello Road and Pimlico Road.

09

Thomas Goode
19 South Audley Street, W1

Great British classics

Asprey
167 New Bond St, W1
⊖ Green Park
℡ 020 7493 6767
asprey.com
⊕ 6/M8

The Conran Shop
Michelin House,
81 Fulham Rd, SW3
⊖ South Kensington
℡ 020 7589 7401
conranshop.co.uk
⊕ 13/F17

David Mellor
4 Sloane Square, SW1
⊖ Sloane Square
℡ 020 7730 4259
davidmellordesign.com
⊕ 14/K15

Divertimenti
33 Marylebone High
St, W1
⊖ Baker Street
℡ 020 7935 0689
divertimenti.co.uk
⊕ 6/L6

Habitat
196 Tottenham Court
Rd, W1
⊖ Goodge Street
℡ 0870 411 5501
habitat.net
⊕ 7/O6

Harvey Nichols
109 Knightsbridge, SW1
⊖ Knightsbridge
℡ 020 7235 5000
⊕ 10/J12

Selfridges
400 Oxford St, W1
⊖ Bond Street
℡ 0870 837 7377
selfridges.co.uk
⊕ 6/K8

Thomas Goode
19 South Audley St, W1
⊖ Bond Street
℡ 020 7499 2823
thomasgoode.co.uk
⊕ 10/L10

Tiffany & Co.
25 Old Bond St, W1
⊖ Green Park
℡ 020 7409 2790
tiffany.com
⊕ 11/N10

09

Porcelain and glassware

Bodo Sperlein
Oxo Tower Wharf,
Barge House St, SE1
⊖ Southwark
ⓒ 020 7633 9413
bodosperlein.com
⊕ 12/T10

Liberty
214 Regent St, W1
⊖ Oxford Circus
ⓒ 020 7734 1234
liberty.co.uk
⊕ 11/O10

Waterford Wedgwood
158 Regent St, W1
⊖ Piccadilly Circus
ⓒ 020 7734 7262
wedgwood.com
⊕ 11/O10

Harrods
87 Brompton Rd, SW1
⊖ Knightsbridge
ⓒ 020 7730 1234
harrods.com
⊕ 10/I13

Vessel
114 Kensington Park
Rd W11
⊖ Notting Hill Gate
ⓒ 020 7727 8001
vesselgallery.com
⊕ 5/B9

William Yeoward
270 Kings Rd, SW3
⊖ Sloane Square
ⓒ 020 7349 7828
williamyeowardcrystal.com
⊕ 14/H17

Retro to contemporary design

**Contemporary
Applied Arts**
2 Percy St, W1
⊖ Tottenham Court Rd
ⓒ 020 7436 2344
caa.org.uk
⊕ 7/O7

Designers Guild
267 Kings Rd, SW3
⊖ Sloane Square
ⓒ 020 7351 5775
designersguild.com
⊕ 14/H17

Ella Doran
46 Cheshire St, E2
⊖ Shoreditch
ⓒ 020 7613 0782
elladoran.co.uk
⊕ Off map

**Contemporary
Ceramics Shop**
7 Marshall St, W1
⊖ Piccadilly Circus
ⓒ 020 7437 7605
cpaceramics.com
⊕ 7/N8

Design Museum Shop
Shad Thames, SE1
⊖ London Bridge
ⓒ 0870 909 9009
designmuseum.org
⊕ 12/Z11

Labour and Wait
18 Cheshire St, E2
⊖ Shoreditch
ⓒ 020 7729 6253
labourandwait.co.uk
⊕ Off map

Individual appeal

Atelier Abigail Ahern
137 Upper St,
Islington, N1
⬤ Angel
ⓒ 020 7354 8181
atelierabigailahern.com
⊕ 4/T2

Ceramica Blue
10 Blenheim Crescent,
W11
⬤ Ladbroke Grove
ⓒ 020 7727 0288
ceramicablue.co.uk
⊕ 5/A8

Kelly Hoppen
175 Fulham Rd, SW3
⬤ Fulham Broadway
ⓒ 020 7351 1910
kellyhoppen.com
⊕ 13/F17

Brickett Davda
342 Kilburn Lane,
Queen's Park, W9
⬤ Queen's Park
ⓒ 020 8969 3239
brickettdavda.com
⊕ Off map

**The Dining
Room Shop**
62 White Hart Lane,
SW13
⬤ Hammersmith
ⓒ 020 8878 1020
thediningroomshop.co.uk
⊕ Off map

Ma Maison
243 Fulham Rd, SW3
⬤ South Kensington
ⓒ 020 7352 1181
mamaison.org.uk
⊕ 13/F17

Cath Kidston
51 Marylebone High
St, W1
⬤ Baker Street
ⓒ 020 7935 6555
cathkidston.co.uk
⊕ 6/L6

Emma Bridgewater
81a Marylebone High
St, W1
⬤ Bond Street
ⓒ 020 7486 6897
emmabridgewater.co.uk
⊕ 6/L6

Nina Campbell
9 Walton St, SW3
⬤ South Kensington
ⓒ 0207 225 1011
ninacampbell.com
⊕ 10/I14

09

Celia Birtwell
71 Westbourne Park
Rd, W2
⬤ Royal Oak
ⓒ 020 7221 0877
⊕ 5/A7

Joanna Wood
48a Pimlico Rd, SW1
⬤ Victoria
ⓒ 020 7730 5064
joannawood.co.uk
⊕ 2/K5

One Deko
111 Commercial St, E1
⬤ Liverpool Street
ⓒ 020 7375 3289
onedeko.co.uk
⊕ 8/Z6

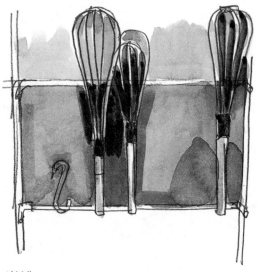

David Mellor
4 Sloane Square, SW1

Kitchen design and utensils

Box3
Unit 53,8 Ada St
Workshops,
Andrews Rd, E8
⊖ Bethnal Green
ⓒ 020 7254 6656
box3.co.uk
⊕ Off map

Holloways of Ludlow
121 Shepherd's Bush
Rd, W6
⊖ Goldhawk Road
ⓒ 020 7602 5757
hollowaysofludlow.co.uk
⊕ Off map

Peter Jones
Sloane Square, SW1
⊖ Sloane Square
ⓒ 020 7730 3434
peterjones.co.uk
⊕ 14/K15

Fired Earth
117 Fulham Rd, SW3
⊖ South Kensington
ⓒ 020 7589 0489
firedearth.com
⊕ 13/F17

Japanese Knife Co
131 Belsize Rd, NW6
⊖ Belsize Park
ⓒ 0870 240 2248
japaneseknifecompany.
com
⊕ Off map

Retrouvius
2a Ravensworth Rd,
NW10
⊖ Kensal Green
ⓒ 020 8960 6060
retrouvius.com
⊕ Off map

Grange
74 Marylebone
High St, W1
⊖ Bond Street
ⓒ 020 7258 9995
aga-web.co.uk
⊕ 6/L6

Mark Wilkinson
126 Holland Park Av,
W11
⊖ Holland Park
ⓒ 020 7727 5814
mwf.com
⊕ 9/A10

Robinson & Cornish
245 Munster Rd, SW6
⊖ Parsons Green
ⓒ 020 7385 9666
robinsonandcornish.
co.uk
⊕ Off map

Heal's
196 Tottenham Court
Rd, W1
⊖ Goodge Street
ⓒ 020 7636 1666
heals.co.uk
⊕ 7/O6

Nicholas Anthony
44 Wigmore St, W1
⊖ Bond Street
ⓒ 020 7935 0177
nicholas-anthony.co.uk
⊕ 6/K8

Skandium
86 Marylebone High
St, W1
⊖ Baker Street
ⓒ 020 7935 2077
skandium.com
⊕ 6/L6

09

See page 9
to scan the
directory

FOODIE EVENTS
AND ONLINE HITS

Le Gavroche
43 Upper Brook St, W1

Previous page: Table dressing
by Lettice Party Design and Catering

The extent of the London food scene doesn't end with excellent restaurants, fine food shops, delicatessens, farmers markets and cookery schools. This chapter will help you to sniff out some of London's other gourmet treats — from star-studded festivals to little-known websites. There are some great blogs, too, for anyone who wants to stay on top of the London culinary scene.

Seasonal food events

The capital's biggest and best food event for the general public is **Taste of London**, which takes place every June in bucolic Regent's Park. The festival, which is a cross between an urban garden party, mobile tasting menu, village fête and celebrity cook-out, is essentially a chance for some of London's best chefs to show off their skills in public.

Up to 50 of them erect mini-kitchens and dole out portions of their signature dishes: you might see, for example, Tom Aikens cooking his famous braised pig's cheek or Michel Roux Jr of Le Gavroche dishing up *saucisson lyonnais en brioche*. In other words, it's a chance to sample a cross section of the best

10

Farmaround, in New Covent Garden Market,
brings seasonal organic food straight from the land

restaurants in town – at a fraction of the price (from £21-£50 per half-day) you would pay if you were actually in these restaurants. Fairgoers stroll between stalls, armed with their Crowns – the festival's currency, tasting as they go. In addition, 150 leading producers exhibit their wares, and there is a demonstration theatre along with other gastronomic shows.

October and November tastings

Another large festival is **Spirit of Christmas**, which takes place every November in the Olympia Exhibition Centre. Food retailers from across Britain exhibit at this shopping jamboree, giving Londoners a chance to sample products that they wouldn't normally encounter. Top chefs hold live demos, and there's a room for the crème de la crème of chocolate makers.

Chocolate lovers, in fact, may wish to make sure that they are in town shortly before Spirit of Christmas, for **London Chocolate Week** in mid- to late-October: this programme of tastings, demos and lectures at chocolate shops and other venues provides a mouth-watering insight into London's dynamic chocolate scene.

Numerous smaller food and wine events take place in London throughout the year; the best way to find out about them is to check with the best fine wine

10

Forman & Field offers home deliveries of fresh,
natural products in The British Isles

and food academies *(see Chapters Six and Seven)*. Also keep an eye out for the events of **Slow Food London**. The London arm of this Italian-based movement isn't as active as some, but it does hold regular tastings and dinners with Slow Food producers.

Home and overseas deliveries

Shopping in London may be fun for visitors, but it can be time-consuming and frustrating for hard-working residents. That's why time-strapped Londoners are increasingly relying on home delivery services from supermarkets, small shops and mail-order websites. Many of the places discussed in other chapters do deliveries (it's always a good idea to ask), but a number of specialist websites are also worth knowing about.

Ocado arranges deliveries on behalf of Waitrose – the best big supermarket in London. The site is easy to use, the service is reliable and deliveries can be arranged in handy one-hour slots. The excellent **Forman & Field** sources artisanal goods from all over the British Isles, including smoked fish and a variety of raw and cured meats. (Try also **Orkney Rose**, which brings hard-to-obtain products from the Orkney Isles in Scotland.) For fresh fish, try **Martin's Seafresh** – this company will transport your order straight from the boat to your door within 48 hours. **Blackface** delivers beef,

10

Abel & Cole
Tel: 0845 262 6262
abel-cole.co.uk

pork, lamb and venison direct from its hill farms in southwest Scotland; for more unusual items, such as ostrich and wild boar, try **Alternative Meats**.

French Gourmet Store stocks a range of delicious French goods, from escargots to *confit de canard*. Unusual Italian produce, such as Campanian buffalo meat, can be purchased from **Esperya**. Or, if you want a full-blown dinner party to arrive piping hot on your doorstep, London's most upmarket takeaway service, **Deliverance**, will deliver a wide range of freshly cooked dishes to your home within 40 minutes.

Organic box schemes

Londoners have become very keen on what is known as organic box schemes, whereby a selection of organic, seasonal fruit and vegetables (as local as possible) is delivered to a customer's door each week, creating a direct link between producer and consumer.

Choice may be limited: some of the smaller schemes operate on a 'you get what you're given' basis. If turnips are in season and you're not fond of turnips, this can be irritating. But other companies, such as **Abel & Cole** – one of the most popular schemes operating in London, offer several different boxes each week, as well as supplementary items such as fish, meat, cheese

10

Fresh & Wild
49 Park Way, NW1

and bread. Organic boxes have proved so popular that supermarkets are getting in on the act: both Sainsbury's and Tesco now offer them. But as one of the points of organic boxes is to favour the small-scale and local and cut out the middlemen, it seems perverse to buy one from a supermarket – especially when there are practical alternatives.

Foodies online

London's food scene is constantly evolving, and the web is a good place for keeping up with the latest developments. Anyone can post a restaurant review on the enormously popular **london-eating.net**; on the basis of these, each restaurant is awarded scores out of ten for food, service, atmosphere and value. It's easy to see why the site is so popular – it's comprehensive, democratic and up-to-the-minute, but it also attracts its share of criticism, mainly on the grounds that there is nothing to stop chefs or restaurant owners from posting reviews to boost their scores.

The London message boards of the international gourmet website **egullet.org** attract some of the capital's most knowledgeable and indefatigable foodies; *The Observer* restaurant critic Jay Rayner is a regular. On the site there are animated discussions about, say, the merits of Gordon Ramsay's various restaurants, or

London Review of Breakfasts
londonreviewofbreakfasts.blogspot.com

the best place to hunt down a jar of Spanish piquillo peppers. The site is particularly useful if you need to plug a hole in your culinary knowledge: post a question like "Where is the best place to eat offal in London?" and suggestions will come flooding back.

The best blogs

London's food lovers are also becoming enthusiastic bloggers. On the enjoyably eccentric **London Review of Breakfasts**, each contributor has a punning pseudonym such as Malcolm Eggs or Phil English. The reviews are written in a mock literary style, but they also provide much useful information. An excellent restaurant blog, consulted by many of London's food insiders, is **Dos Hermanos**, the account of two brothers' intrepid trawl through London's restaurant scene.

10

Seasonal food events and tastings

BBC Good Food Show
Olympia Exhibition Centre
Hammersmith Rd, W14
londonbbcgood
foodshow.com

London Chocolate Week
chocolate-week.co.uk

**Speciality and
Fine Food Fair**
Olympia Exhibition Centre
Hammersmith Rd, W14
specialityandfine/
foodfairs.co.uk

**International Food
and Drink Exhibition**
ExCeL London,
Royal Victoria Dock, E16
ife.co.uk

Taste of London
Regent's Park, W11
tasteoflondon.co.uk

Spirit of Christmas
Olympia Exhibition Centre
Hammersmith Road, W14
spiritofchristmasfair.co.uk

Home and overseas deliveries

Alernative Meats
(European Union)
℡ 0844 545 6070
alternativemeats.co.uk

Foodfullstop
(United Kingdom)
℡ 0870 383 0122
foodfullstop.com

Martin's Seafresh
(United Kingdom)
℡ 01637 806 103
martins-seafresh.co.uk

Blackface
(United Kingdom)
℡ 01387 730 326
blackface.co.uk

Forman & Field
(United Kingdom)
℡ 020 8221 3939
formanandfield.com

Ocado
(United Kingdom)
℡ 0845 399 1122
ocado.com

Deliverance
(London)
℡ 0844 477 1111
deliverance.co.uk

French Gourmet Store
*(UK, EU, US, Canada,
Far East, Australasia)*
frenchgourmetstore.com

Olives Et Al
(International)
℡ 01258 474 300
olivesetal.com

Esperya
(European Union)
℡ 00800 280 52003
esperya.com

GoodnessDirect
(UK, EU)
℡ 0871 871 6611
goodnessdirect.co.uk

The Olive Trail
(Worldwide)
℡ 01373 471 836
theolivetrail.com

Orkney Rose
(London)
℗ 0560 115 5643
orkneyrose.com

Seasoned Pioneers
(International)
℗ 0800 068 2348
seasonedpioneers.co.uk

Tregida Smokehouse
(United Kingdom)
℗ 01840 261 785
tregidasmokehouse.co.uk

Catering companies

Cooks & Partners
℗ 020 7731 5282
cooksandpartners.co.uk

Nomad
℗ 020 7261 1555
nomadlondon.co.uk

Simply Gourmet
℗ 020 7277 7200
gourmet-canape.com

Lettice Party Design and Catering
℗ 020 7820 1161
letticeparty.com

Rhubarb Food Design
℗ 020 8812 3200
rhubarb.net

Zafferano
℗ 020 7249 4455
zafferano.co.uk

Organic box schemes

Abel & Cole
℗ 0845 262 6262
abel-cole.co.uk

Farmaround
℗ 020 7627 8066
farmaround.co.uk

The Organic Delivery Company
℗ 020 7739 8181
organicdelivery.co.uk

Foodies online and the best blogs

Dos Hermanos
majbros-blogspot.com

London Review of Breakfasts
londonreviewofbreakfasts.
blogspot.com

Slow Food London
slowfoodlondon.com

eGullet
egullet.org

Mouthfuls
mouthfulsfood.com

Why Organic
whyorganic.org

London Eating
london-eating.net

Ripelondon
ripelondon.typepad.com

10

See page 9
to scan the
directory

11

INDEX

Page numbers in italics refer to chapter directories

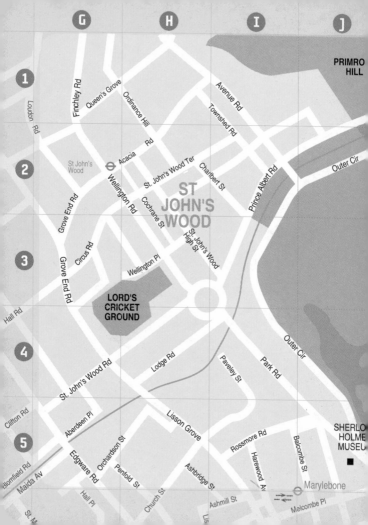

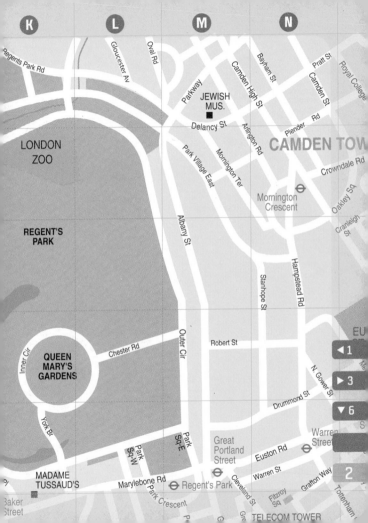

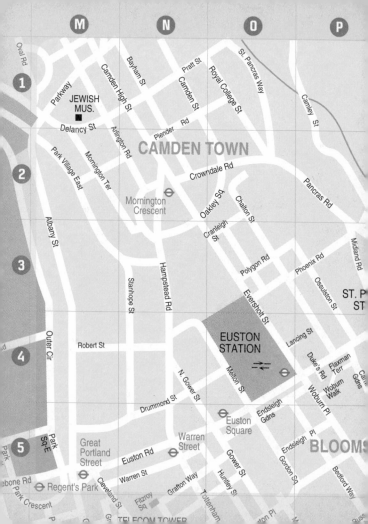

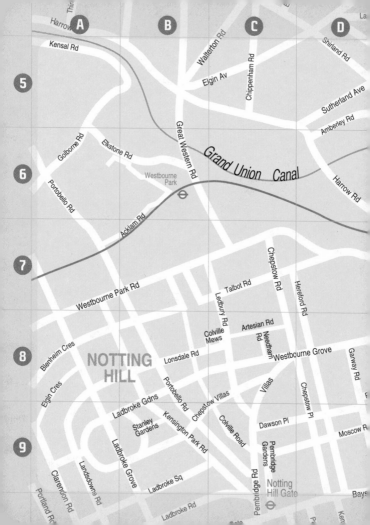

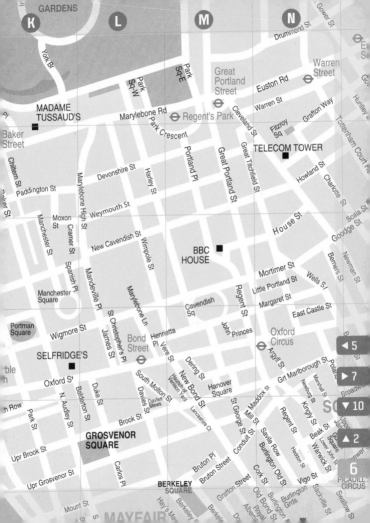

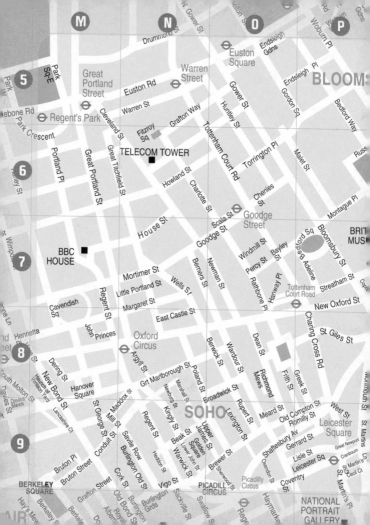

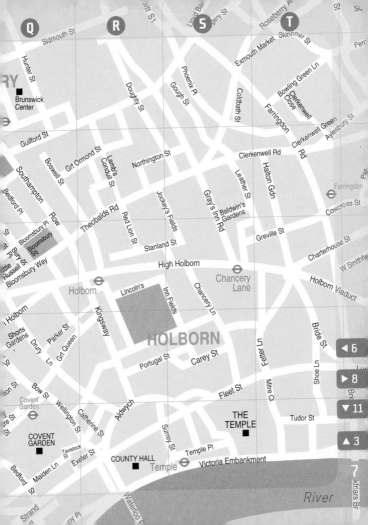

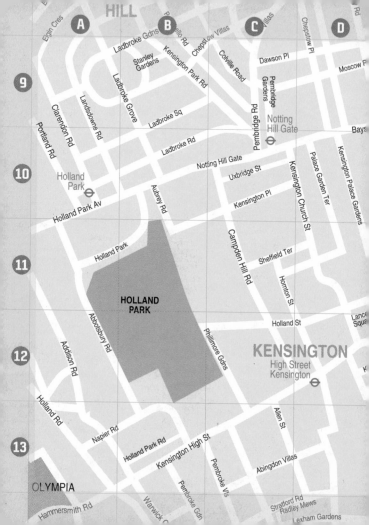

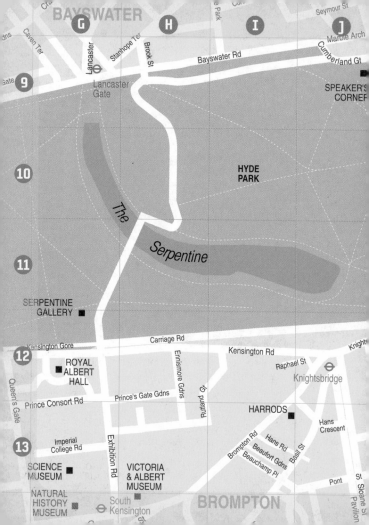

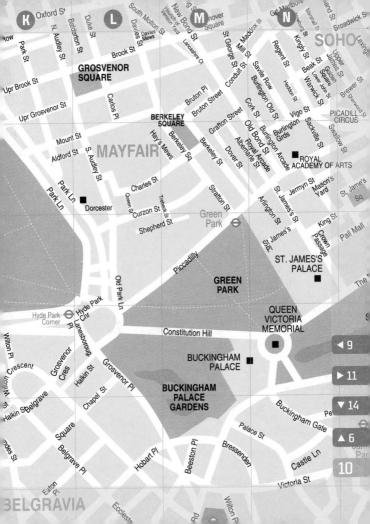

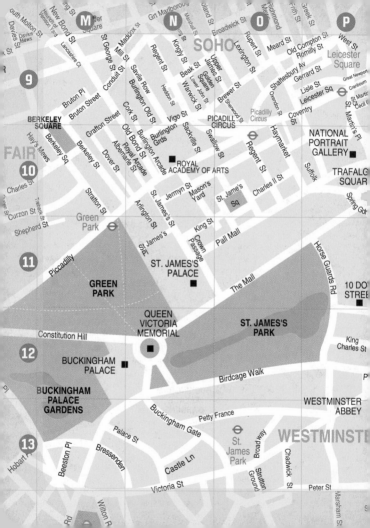

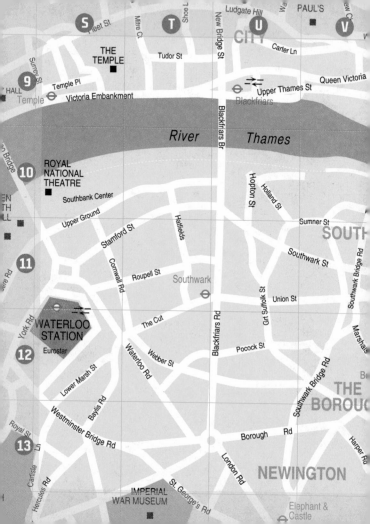

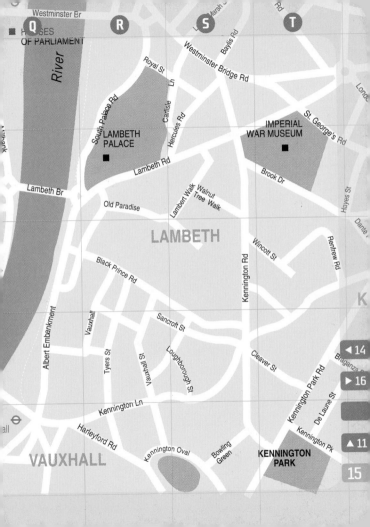

Westminster Br

Q **R** **S** **T**

HOUSES
OF PARLIAMENT

River

Westminster Bridge Rd
Baylis Rd

Royal St
Carlisle Ln
Hercules Rd

South Palace Rd

LAMBETH
PALACE

IMPERIAL
WAR MUSEUM

St. George's Rd

Londo

Lambeth Rd

Lambeth Br

Brook Dr

Hayes St

Dante

Old Paradise

Lambert Walk
Walnut
Tree Walk

LAMBETH

Wincott St

Black Prince Rd

Kennington Rd

Renfrew Rd

K

Albert Embankment

Vauxhall

Sancroft St

Tyers St

Vauxhall St

Loughborough St

Cleaver St

◄ 14

► 16

Braganza

Kennington Park Rd

De Laune St

Kennington Ln

▲ 11

Harleyford Rd

VAUXHALL

all

Kennington Oval

Bowling
Green

Kennington Pk

**KENNINGTON
PARK**

15

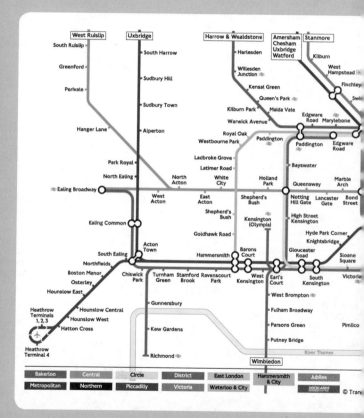

LONDON U

West Ruislip
- South Ruislip
- Greenford
- Perivale
- Hanger Lane
- Park Royal
- North Ealing
- Ealing Broadway
- Ealing Common
- South Ealing
- Northfields
- Boston Manor
- Osterley
- Hounslow East
- Heathrow Terminals 1, 2, 3
- Hounslow Central
- Hounslow West
- Hatton Cross
- Heathrow Terminal 4

Uxbridge
- South Harrow
- Sudbury Hill
- Sudbury Town
- Alperton
- North Acton
- West Acton
- East Acton
- Acton Town
- Chiswick Park
- Turnham Green
- Stamford Brook
- Ravenscourt Park
- Gunnersbury
- Kew Gardens
- Richmond

Harrow & Wealdstone
- Harlesden
- Willesden Junction
- Kensal Green
- Queen's Park
- Kilburn Park
- Maida Vale
- Warwick Avenue
- Royal Oak
- Westbourne Park
- Ladbroke Grove
- Latimer Road
- White City
- Shepherd's Bush
- Shepherd's Bush
- Goldhawk Road
- Hammersmith
- West Kensington
- Barons Court
- Earl's Court
- West Brompton
- Fulham Broadway
- Parsons Green
- Putney Bridge

Amersham / Chesham / Uxbridge / Watford
Stanmore
- Kilburn
- West Hampstead
- Finchley
- Swis

- Edgware Road
- Marylebone
- Paddington
- Paddington
- Edgware Road
- Bayswater
- Holland Park
- Queensway
- Marble Arch
- Notting Hill Gate
- Lancaster Gate
- Bond Street
- High Street Kensington
- Kensington (Olympia)
- Hyde Park Corner
- Knightsbridge
- Gloucester Road
- Sloane Square
- South Kensington
- Victoria
- Pimlico

River Thames

Wimbledon

Bakerloo	Central	Circle	District	East London	Hammersmith & City	Jubilee
Metropolitan	Northern	Piccadilly	Victoria	Waterloo & City	DOCKLANDS	

© Tran

ERGROUND

Edgware
Belsize Park
Chalk Farm
Camden Town
Mornington Crescent
Great Portland Street
Euston
Warren Street
Euston Square
Goodge Street
Holborn
Tottenham Court Road
Leicester Square
Charing Cross
Embankment
Charing Cross
Waterloo
Southwark
Waterloo East
Lambeth North
Borough
Morden
Elephant & Castle
Piccadilly Circus
Mansion House
Blackfriars
Temple
Westminster

High Barnet
Mill Hill East
Kentish Town
Holloway Road
Caledonian Road
King's Cross
St. Pancras
Angel
Farringdon
Barbican
Russell Square
Chancery Lane
St. Paul's
Cannon Street
Covent Garden

Cockfosters
Walthamstow Central
Arsenal
Finsbury Park
Highbury & Islington
Old Street
Liverpool Street
Moorgate
Bank
Aldgate
Monument
Tower Hill
Fenchurch Street
London Bridge
Bermondsey
Canada Water

Bethnal Green
Shoreditch
Aldgate East
Whitechapel
Shadwell
Tower Gateway
Wapping
Rotherhithe

Mile End
Stepney Green
Limehouse
Westferry

Epping
Hainault
Barking
Upminster
Beckton
Lewisham

Stratford

New Cross
New Cross Gate

River Thames

UNDERGROUND

London Travel Information
020 7222 1234
Textphone
020 7918 3015
24 hours

LTM CD(b) 03.01   Reg. user No. 01/3529   www.transportforlondon.gov.uk

OTHER TITLES IN THE AUTHENTIK COLLECTION

Europe
Chic London
Artistik London

Gourmet Paris
Chic Paris
Artistik Paris

FORTHCOMING AUTHENTIK GUIDES – SPRING 2008

North America
Gourmet New York
Chic New York
Artistik New York

Europe
Barcelona
Berlin
Milan
Prague

Asia
Beijing

FORTHCOMING WINE ROADBOOKS – AUTUMN 2008

France
Bordeaux
Burgundy
Champagne
Loire Valley

Italy
Tuscany

Spain
Rioja

North America
Napa Valley
Sonoma County

Visit www.authentikbooks.com
to find out more about **AUTHENTIK** ® titles

K

William Skidelsky

William is a London-based writer and editor specializing in food, books and culture. As an avid observer and chronicler of the London culinary scene, he is well equipped to pen the perfect one-stop-guide for any discerning gourmet in London. William is currently deputy editor of *Prospect* magazine.

Alain Bouldouyre

Gentleman artist Alain Bouldouyre captures in his fine line drawings what our *Gourmet London* author conjures up in words – the quintessence of the city. Art director for *Senso* magazine, and author/illustrator of numerous travel books, Alain fast tracks around the world in hand-stitched loafers – a paintbox and sketch pad his most precious accessories.

COMMERCIAL LICENSING
Authentik illustrations, text and listings are available for commercial licensing at www.authentikartwork.com

ORIGINAL ARTWORK
All signed and numbered original illustrations by Alain Bouldouyre published in this book are available for sale. Original artwork by Alain Bouldouyre is delivered framed with a certificate of authenticity.

CUSTOM-MADE EDITIONS
Authentik books make perfect, exclusive gifts for personal or corporate purposes.

Special editions, including personalized covers, excerpts from existing titles and corporate imprints, can be custom produced.

All enquiries should be addressed to Wilfried LeCarpentier at wl@authentikbooks.com

NOTES

K